WITH I
SO LIGHT.

The Story of the Queen Pit Explosions,
Haydock. December 1868 and July 1869.

By
Ian Winstanley

[signature: Ian Winstanley]

Published by
PICKS PUBLISHING
83, Greenfields Crescent,
Ashton-in-Makerfield.
Nr. Wigan.
Lancashire.
WN4 8QY.

Telephone. (0942) 723675.

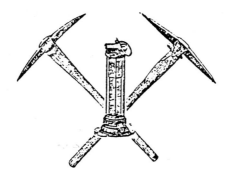

ISBN 0 9516843 0 2

Photoset & Printed by:
Willow Printing (0925) 222449/228524

ACKNOWLEDGEMENTS.

My grateful thanks for the help and encouragement in writing this book go to the dedicated and cheerful staffs of the St. Helens Local History Library and Archive and Wigan Reference Library and Wigan Record Office. I am also indebted to Wigan Mining and Technical Collage Library, The Salford Mining Museum, Buile Hill, British Coal, Geoff Simm, Ulrich West and the Vicars of Ashton, Haydock and Parr. I would like to record my thanks to Mr. M. Worsley and "Northern Conveyors" for their generous sponsorship.

The 'auld 'uns of Yick' also gave me much interesting information and without all this help the book would not have gone to press.

I.G.W. September, 1990.

Lines written after the 1868 explosion explosion.

With hearts so light they left their homes upon that fateful day,
They little thought what would occur before the night's return;
Our life is quite uncertain, as plainly we may see,
One moment we are in blooming health, the next in eternity.

To the memory of the men and boys who set out
with hearts so light on those fateful mornings
and to my friend Brian.

SKETCH MAP SHOWING THE POSITION OF HAYDOCK.

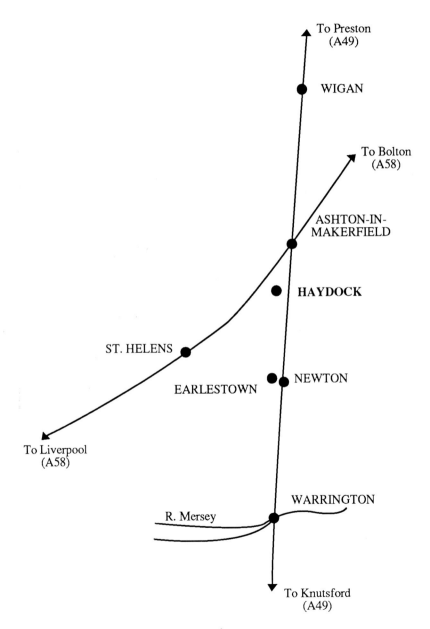

SKETCH MAP OF HAYDOCK.

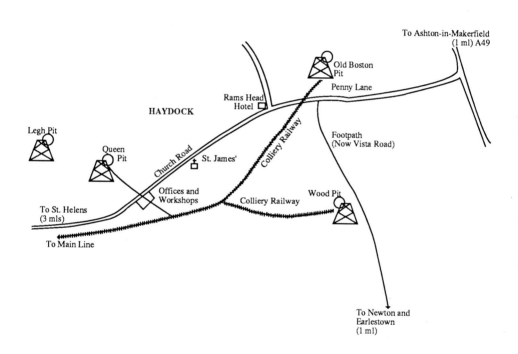

To Ashton-in-Makerfield
(1 ml) A49

Old Boston Pit

Penny Lane

Rams Head Hotel

HAYDOCK

Footpath
(Now Vista Road)

Legh Pit

Queen Pit

Church Road

St. James'

Colliery Railway

Offices and Workshops

Colliery Railway

Wood Pit

To St. Helens
(3 mls)

To Main Line

To Newton and
Earlestown
(1 ml)

AUTHORS' NOTES.

This project started some years ago when I realised that all the pits in Haydock, that I had known as a lad, had gone for ever. In trying to increase my own knowledge it was soon found that very little had been written about the pits and mining in the Haydock area. My purpose in putting pen to paper is to record what happened in the village in 1868-9 and to try to return the reader to those days. In putting this account together, I have used local press accounts of the time and other contemporary sources.

The explosions at the colliery must be viewed in the context of the state of mining at the time in the full flow of the Industrial Revolution. It was a new, fast growing industry. The demand for coal was very great, railways and the machinery of industry were all powered by steam and the new industrial processes to manufacture iron and steel required vast amounts of coal. In the coalfields of the country new pits were being sunk almost weekly and the rich seams of coal that lay deep underground were being exploited by the best that the mining technology of the day had to offer.

Mistakes were made and new techniques were evolved often at the price of the colliers lives. The Victorian public conscience was stirred by the reports of the explosions and disasters and by 1850 the Mining Inspectorate was set up with Government Inspectors appointed to look after a large and growing number of collieries in their areas. They made their first report in 1850.

In Lancashire the number of pits had risen dramatically and the Inspector was overwhelmed with work. Much of his time was spent investigating accidents that had resulted in the loss of life, not in great explosions but in the day to day running of the mines that cost the lives of colliers and other workers almost as a daily occurrence.

The Government Inspectors had no powers of compulsion on the mine owners and had to operate a system of arbitration, which was always worked in the owners' favour. Mr Higson, the Inspector for Lancashire, lost a case of arbitration some little time before concerning the closure of a St. Helens colliery and he was only too well aware of his weak position in such circumstances.

I have made no critical comments on the events but I have attempted to report fully on what was said at the time by the people directly involved and to tell the story of what happened in those distant days. Some of the language used in the book is archaic and I make no apology. It gives the flavour of the time and the tense atmosphere, particularly at the inquest into the July explosion, is brought into sharp focus.

The events in the village of Haydock in 1868 and 1869 raised wider issues of National interest in the state of mining at the time and I have used these accounts, often verbatim, to present a contemporary account of what happened in Haydock in those distant years and wherever possible I have used the names of the people involved in my account of the events, often dramatic, that took place in the village so long ago.

I.G.W. September, 1990.

CONTENTS.

GLOSSARY OF THE TERMS
USED IN THE BOOK.

AFTERDAMP.

After an explosion the mine was filled with the products of the burning gas. These were mainly carbon monoxide (CO) which is poisonous and carbon dioxide (CO_2) which is suffocating.

BLOWER.

Large amounts of methane gas is trapped under pressure in the coal and will seep out. If a large reservoir is broken into then it will blow out of the coal.

BRATTICE.

Fresh air was directed to the ends of the workings by constructing wooden frames down the centre of the tunnel and covering the frame with thick canvas brattice cloth that was nailed to the frames.

BROW.

See downbrow and up brow.

BANKSMAN or BROWMAN.

The man at the surface who was in charge of the pit bank. He was responsible for loading and unloading the cage and for signalling to the engineman who was responsible for winding the cage.

CAGE.

A crude lift that was wound up and down the shaft carrying men and materials.

COALFACE.

The place where the coal was exposed and the colliers won it.

COLLIER.

The skilled man who worked at the coalface and actually got the coal.

COLLIERY.

The sit at the surface that includes all the building, rail ways and headgear.

CUT THROUGH.
> A short tunnel connecting two roads.

DATALLER.
> A man who was employed to do service work in the mine and was paid by the day.

DELF.
> A Lancashire term to describe a coal seam.

DOOR TENTER.
> See tenter.

DRAWER.
> A person who was employed by the collier to take full tubs of coal from the workplace to the haulage and bring back empty tubs.

FIREDAMP.
> Methane gas that comes naturally from the coal. It is inflammable but when mixed with air it becomes explosive.

FIREMAN.
> An official who is in charge of a district of the mine.

MINE.
> The name given in Lancashire to a coal seam.

PIT.
> The shaft from the surface to the workings.

PIT BANK.
> The top of the shaft and the area immediately around it.

PIT EYE.
> The area around the bottom of the shaft.

PLACE.
> The work place at the coal face where the collier worked.

STOPPINGS.
> Walls built across the roads and tunnels that would seal an area of the mine.

TENTER.
> Someone who looked after something, e.g. furnace tenter, door tenter and pony tenter.

UNDERLOOKER.
> An official in charge of the mine and supervising the firemen.

INTRODUCTION.

The Queen Pit at Haydock was owned by Richard Evans & Co., the local coal owner. He was previously a publisher, who lived in Paternoster Row, London and had decided to move to the north to invest in the booming coal industry. He had bought a share in the Edge Green colliery at Ashton-in-Makerfield in 1829 and as time went on, his business expanded and became responsible for all the mining operations in Haydock. The Queen Pit was not a new colliery. It had been mentioned in the 1830's and was sunk to mine the rich seams that lay below Haydock, the Ravenhead Main Delf Six Foot Mine, and the Wigan Nine Foot Mine.

Following the Hartley Colliery disaster in the north-east coalfield in 1864, legislation had insisted that every colliery should have two shafts. One, through which the clean air passed to the workings, was called the downcast and the other that carried the foul air to the atmosphere, was called the upcast shaft. Usually these two shafts were close together but at this colliery the downcast was known as Queen Pit and the upcast shaft as Legh Pit with about a quarter of a mile between them.

By 1868, underground development work was taking place to open up the coal seams. To us today, the methods that were used may seem primitive but every care was taken with regard to the safety of the men by the coal owners. The engineers and colliers of the time were working at the frontiers of a modern technology and, as with the railways, it was not until a disaster occurred, that the dangers became known to mining men and to the general public. Only then was there pressure for legislation to make the job safer. The drafting and enactment of such legislation often took years

The dangers of methane gas, called firedamp by the miners, had been known for a long time and the practice of dealing with the problem had been improved since the very early days of mining coal when a man, covered with wet sacking known as the 'penitent', would be the first to go down the shaft in the morning and crawl through the workings with a long lighted torch held near the roof to burn off the gas that had collected overnight. The wet sacking was to prevent him getting burnt. This was not always successful.

Although Messrs Evans & Co, had a good reputation and record for safety, there had been accidents and deaths caused by the explosion of firedamp at the colliery before the first major explosion in December 1868. An account of these is given in the Report of the Mines Inspectors and in the mining literature of the time.

In March 1867, an explosion was reported in the local press in which a man died and several others were badly hurt. The men were working in the Ravenhead Main Delf Mine about five in the morning, when two colliers fired a shot to bring down the coal. It was usual at this time to fire two shots at the same time and the charges were made up of gunpowder. One of the shots misfired and the fuse ignited the brattice cloth which in turn set fire to the coal. With the brattice destroyed, the ventilation was interrupted and there was a build up of gas which was ignited by the fire. This led to an explosion in which eight men were burnt and one died.

The officials of the colliery who worked underground, the underlookers, quickly got the injured men out of the mine and the local doctor, Dr. Twyford, treated them at the surface. John Dickenson, William Grimshaw, John Mercer, Henry Forshaw, William Wedgewood, Edward Hazeldene and John Merricks were all burnt to some degree and James Parr was so badly burnt that he died the following day.

The inquest into the death of James Parr was held a few days later at Mr. James Greenall's public house, the Waggon and Horses, in Clipsley Lane, Haydock under the direction of Mr. C. E. Driffield, the County Coroner.

Mr. Isaac Billinge, the manager of the mine, said that he was twenty to thirty yards from the explosion supervising some men who were building a wall when the force of the blast blew him off his feet.

John Wilcock of Millfield Lane, Haydock and John Dene were the men who fired the shots and they told the court how the shot had misfired and set fire to the brattice cloth.

The Coroner and the jury heard the evidence and returned a verdict of accidental death on James Parr aged twenty years, a collier of Haydock.

The same mining practices were continued, the use of brattice to direct the flow of air round the workings and the use of slow-match fuses to fire gunpowder charges to bring down the coal.

The stage was set for the two terrible explosions that were to claim the lives of almost eighty men within the next four years including that of John Wilcox, the man who fired the shot. He was to die in the explosion in December 1868 along with John Merricks who was burnt, and twenty four other men and boys.

THE EXPLOSION OF 30th. DECEMBER 1868.

The village of Haydock, which is seven miles from Wigan and three from St. Helens, was described at the time as being clean and neat with well trimmed hedges. It was a long straggling village with rows of terraced miner's cottages along the main road that ran through the village. Each cottage had a well tended garden behind the low wall that fronted the road. The well cultivated farmland ran from behind behind the houses almost to the pit banks and to an observer, the only evidence of how the village earned it's bread were the many pit headgears that overlooked the cottages.

Queen Pit was one of seven collieries in the village owned by Richard Evans & Co. and was situated a few yards from the colliery offices at the top of the village. The pits were known collectively as the Haydock Collieries and employed about fifteen hundred men in the 1860'ties.

The General Manager of the Haydock Collieries was Mr. John Chadwick, a well respected man of great mining experience. The underlooker of the Queen Pit was Mr. Isaac Billinge who was in charge of the Wigan Nine Foot Mine and he was directly responsible to Mr. Chadwick. The Evans Company had a good reputation and it was generally agreed that they spared no expense for the safety of their workforce in the collieries.

There were two seams worked at the colliery but development work was in an early stage and coal had been extracted for only about eighteen months to two years. The two seams were the Ravenhead Main Delf Six Foot Mine and the Wigan Nine Foot Mine. The latter is where the explosion took place and it was two hundred and sixty yards from the surface.

The coal in the mine where the explosion occurred was hard and had to be blasted down by gunpowder for the colliers to make a living. The colliers were responsible for making their own charges and for setting them. They bought their own powder and made up the charges in their own homes. The charges were laid by drilling a hole in the coal and ramming in the charge. This was common practice in the district and had lead to many serious accidents in the collier's homes often with fatal results. By the Law of the time, the fireman should fire the shot but in practice, many of the colliers fired their own but only after the fireman had inspected the workplace. This was the general practice throughout the coalfield and the practice had led to many accidents that were recorded in the Reports of the Inspectors of Mines. The burning fuse or the flash of the explosion igniting the gas that was be present. This resulted in either devastating explosions or more usually, in the gas igniting and inflicting severe burns on the men that were in the vicinity

As was customary at the time, the mine was ventilated by a furnace being continually alight at the bottom of the upcast shaft which was known as Legh Pit and was about four hundred yards from the Queen Pit which was the downcast shaft. As the hot air passed up Legh Pit, cold, fresh air was drawn down Queen Pit and directed to the workings of the mine by walls, called stoppings, which were built across the tunnels and by air-doors that could be opened to allow the passage of men and materials but were generally kept closed. Men, materials and coal were wound at Queen Pit.

To get the fresh air to the coalface and working places, the narrow tunnel was divided in two by a wooden frame onto which was nailed a thick canvas cloth that was tarred, called brattice cloth. The air flow was kept as close as possible to the coalface so that the men could breath and any gas that came from the coal could be carried away up the upcast shaft.

Work began at the colliery at six in the morning and although there were forty employees, on that fateful morning, only twenty three man and boys descended into the Wigan Nine Foot workings. As the work got under way, Mr. Billinge made his inspection of the mine as was required by the Special Rules of the Colliery. He found nothing he regarded as dangerous. The ventilation was in good order and the men were getting on with their difficult, dangerous work in their usual professional manner.

There was an incident below ground that morning that saved the life of a man named Flanagan. He was a collier and his son, John was his drawer. Early in the shift, Joseph Greenall, the fireman, caught Flanagan snr. smoking which was against the Rules of the Colliery and he immediately ordered him to the surface and told him to go home. Smoking in the pit was not uncommon at the time and there are many recorded cases in the Magistrates Courts of the time. Both John Flanagan and Joseph Greenall were killed in the subsequent explosion.

It was shortly before noon that other men down the pit noticed that the ventilation had altered and when they went to investigate they found that an explosion had taken place. They left the mine as quickly as possible. They would be only too well aware of the dangers of afterdamp, the poisonous gases that are left in the mine after an explosion and lethal in the confined spaces of the workings. When the explosion occurred there was little noise and the three hundred men who were in the Ravenhead Mine knew little of the event. All the damage was confined to about five hundred yards of the workings in the Wigan Nine Foot Mine.

The Explosion

John Chadwick and Isaac Billinge were both above ground when the explosion occurred and were told of the event by those that had escaped from the pit. Immediately they went to the pit head and started to organise a rescue party. Fortunately the headgear and the cage were undamaged and there was no hindrance to the rescuers to go below ground.

As soon as they reached the pit bottom they found three survivors who were badly injured and sent them to the surface where, by this time, Dr. Twyford had arrived to attend to the them. Peter Marsh aged thirteen years was badly burnt and died at six a.m. on Friday. John Flanagan aged eleven years was suffering from the effects of afterdamp and died the same day at home and Robert Fletcher Room aged nineteen years was badly burnt and died later at home.

It was too dangerous for the rescue party to enter the workings until they had restored the ventilation. This was difficult and dangerous work but they made good progress and entered the workings about an hour an a half later. They found another survivor, Hugh Arnold. His place of work was not ventilated by the flow of air from the main workings. After the explosion, instead of trying to make his way out of the mine, he sat in his workplace moaning and probably suffering from shock. It was in this state that the rescuers found him. He was taken to the surface and recovered to give evidence at the inquest.

The rescue parties worked on, replacing the stoppings, repairing the broken air-doors and erecting new bratticing that had been blown down by the force of the explosion. The violence of the explosion could clearly be seen, tubs and waggons had been smashed and rails torn up. The centre of the blast was thought to be about two hundred and fifty yards from the pit eye.

As the bodies were found, they were given a number and moved to a position near the pit eye from where it would be an easy matter to raise then to the surface by the cage. The teams worked on throughout the night in relays and by seven in the evening seventeen bodies had been recovered. By Thursday morning all the workings had been searched and twenty three bodies recovered.

During the rescue operations Mr. Billinge became a victim of the afterdamp while he was leading a party. He was taken home and recovered to give evidence at the inquest.

As was usual in the situation, the bodies were brought to the surface at night in an attempt to keep them from the eyes of friends, relations and the curious who had gathered at the pit bank. The works carpenters had constructed a wooden shed to house the dead. It had taken one and a half hours to construct and contained raised platforms on which the dead were laid out after they had been washed and their clothes bundled at the foot of the platform.

The friends and relatives were admitted on Friday to make their identification of the dead and Mr. C. E. Driffield, the County Coroner, had been contacted and set up court in the Waggon and Horses Hotel in Clipsley Lane, where the evidence of identification was heard. When the Coroner was satisfied on the evidence of identification the bodies were released for burial.

Most of the victims were buried at St. James C. of E., Haydock, St. Thomas's C. of E., Ashton-in-Makerfield, Parr C. of E. and the cemetery at Newton-le-Willows. Mr. Evans ordered that the coffins should be made by the Company's carpenters in the workshops under the direction of the foreman, Mr. John Smith, and that only the finest quality oak should be used so that there should be no complaint from the families.

Some sad stories emerged as the story was pieced together by those who got out of the mine. Henry Hindley, aged twelve years, was on holiday from school and had been taken down the pit by his father, Joseph, to watch him at work. both were dreadfully burnt and died in the explosion.

There had been an explosion at the Hindley Green colliery,a few miles outside Wigan, two or three weeks before and two men who had worked there, but whose names are not recorded, had refused to go down the pit again and had sought employment at Queen Pit. Both were killed in the Wigan Nine Foot mine.

Pewfall Pit, another of the Haydock Collieries, had been flooded due to the excavations that were taking place for the Lancashire Union Railway which was under construction and the whole of the workforce of the colliery, some two hundred men, were thrown out of work. Three of the men named Marsh, John, Joseph and John jur., had taken employment at Queen Pit and for some of them this was their first day at their new work.

Joseph Mercer was working with several other men in Yate's Level. When the explosion occurred all the men left the district and got out of the pit but he stayed behind thinking that the noise of the explosion was that of a shot being fired. He died from the effects of afterdamp. News of his death was brought to Mrs. Mercer at their home in Clipsley Lane. She went upstairs, very upset at the news. A second messenger came to the house to say that her husband was not dead afterall. When she was told this she jumped for joy and unfortunately fell down the stairs and broke her arm. It is not recorded what happened to Mrs. Mercer when she finally learned that her husband was numbered with the dead.

Those victims that had died from the effects of the afterdamp were said to have serene expressions on their faces and were easily identified but identification was difficult on the others who were badly burnt and so many of the victims had taken the full force of the explosion that they were badly mutilated. One poor widow was in doubt about the identity of her husband for a long time but she finally made a positive identification from a slight mark on the body. A large crowd had gathered outside the shed and they heard the heart rending sobs from the relatives as they recognised their loved ones.

As soon as the news of the explosion reached the offices of Richard Evans, Her Majesties Inspector of Mines for the area, Mr. Peter Higson, was contacted by telegram. Mr. Higson arrived at the colliery about nine thirty p.m. with his son who was the Assistant Inspector. Mr. William Pickard, the miners agent, also arrived at the colliery. An investigating party of these men, Mr. Chadwick, Mr. Evans. Mr. Clarke, who was the mining engineer to Sir Robert Gerard who owned mines in Ashton-in-Makerfield, and Mr. Glover, who was the mining engineer to Mr. W. J. Legh M.P. who was the lessor of the Queen Pit, descended the pit in an effort to find out what had caused the explosion.

There were theories that part of the brattice work had been disturbed by a fall of roof and the resulting interruption of the ventilation had caused a build up of gas. Several shots were found to have been placed in position but there was no evidence that these shots had been fired.

The day before the explosion, Mr. Chadwick had made a full inspection of the workings and he had found them in excellent order. A correspondent to the Wigan Observer, whose name is unrecorded, expressed great surprise at the accident since he had visited the mine on two occasions and reported to the paper, "that the ventilation was so good it quite chilled me through".

The firemen had completed their inspections on the Wednesday morning and had reported nothing out of the ordinary in the mine. Both firemen were killed in the explosion. The head fireman, Mr. Greenall, was found some distance from his lamp and it was thought that he had been struck down while racing away from the flames that would have swept through the workings as he tried to make his escape by running for his life.

Mr. P. Higson commented on the devastating effect of the explosion, not in the number killed, but in the fact that it killed twenty four out of the twenty six men and boys that were working in the district. The seventeen men that were killed left left seventeen widows and fifty four children fatherless.

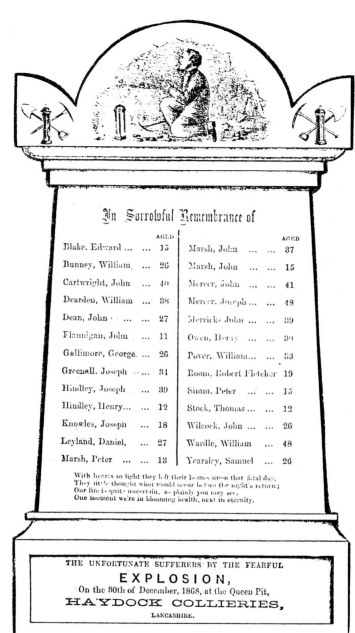

In Sorrowful Remembrance of

	AGED			AGED
Blake, Edward	15	Marsh, John		37
Bunney, William	26	Marsh, John		15
Cartwright, John	40	Mercer, John		41
Dearden, William	38	Mercer, Joseph		48
Dean, John	27	Merricks John		39
Flannigan, John	11	Owen, Henry		39
Gallimore, George	26	Pover, William		53
Greenall, Joseph	31	Room, Robert Fletcher	19
Hindley, Joseph	39	Simm, Peter		15
Hindley, Henry	12	Stock, Thomas		12
Knowles, Joseph	18	Wilcock, John		26
Leyland, Daniel	27	Wardle, William		48
Marsh, Peter	13	Yearsley, Samuel		26

With hearts so light they left their homes upon that fatal day,
They little thought what would occur before the night's return;
Our life is quite uncertain, as plainly you may see,
One moment we're in blooming health, next in eternity.

THE UNFORTUNATE SUFFERERS BY THE FEARFUL
EXPLOSION,
On the 30th of December, 1868, at the Queen Pit,
HAYDOCK COLLIERIES,
LANCASHIRE.

The Unfortunate Sufferers, December 1868.

THE VICTIMS OF THE DECEMBER EXPLOSION.

BLAKE Edward. aged 15 years.
A drawer who lived in Blackbrook, Haydock and was buried at Parr St. Peter's 3rd. January.

BUNNEY William aged 26 years.
A married dataller of Haydock.

CARTWRIGHT John aged 40 years.
A collier of Old Fold, Haydock who left a wife and five children.

DEARDEN William aged 38 years.
A married collier with no children of Toll Bar, Haydock and was buried at Parr St. Peter's 3rd January.

DEAN John aged 27 years.
A collier of Toll Bar, Haydock who was brought out of the pit alive but died later.

GALLIMORE George aged 26 years.
A married collier of Blackbrook, Haydock, who left four children.

GREENALL Joseph aged 34 years.
A fireman who left a wife. He was a Haydock man.

HINDLEY Joseph aged 39 years.
A collier of Penny Lane, Haydock who left a wife and six children. Another son, Henry was killed in the explosion.

HINDLEY Henry aged 12 years.
Joseph was his father and he had taken him with him to watch him work.

KNOWLES Daniel aged 27 years.
A drawer of Ashton-in-Makerfield

LEYLAND Daniel aged 27 years.
A collier of Stone Row, Haydock who left a wife and four children.

MARSH Peter   aged 13 years.

>He lived in Ashton-in-Makerfield and was brought out of the pit alive but very badly burnt and died later.

MARSH John   aged 37 years.

>A collier of Old Fold, Haydock who left a widow and four children. He was uncle to John Marsh aged 15 years.

MARSH John   aged 15 years.

>A drawer of Old Fold, Haydock. John Marsh was his uncle and was buried at Parr St. Peter's 3rd January.

MERCER John   aged 48 years.

>A dataller of Earlestown who left a wife and four children.

MERRICKS John   aged 30 years.

>He left a wife and four children. A collier of New Boston, Haydock.

OWEN Henry   aged 30 years.

>He left a wife and four children. A collier of New Boston, Haydock.

POVER William   aged 33 years.

>A collier of Toll Bar, Haydock who left a wife and four children. He was buried at Parr St. Peter's 3rd January.

ROOM Robert Fletcher   aged 19 years.

>Twenty-eight Row , Haydock who lived with Hugh Arnold. He was brought to the surface alive but badly injured and died later.

SIMM Peter   aged 15 years.

>A pony driver of Clipsley Lane, Haydock.

STOCK Thomas   aged 26 years.

>A drawer of Blackbrook, Haydock.

WILCOCK John   aged 26 years.

>A collier of Millfield Lane, Haydock. who left a wife.

WARDLE William   aged 48 years.

> A married man. Collier of Stone Row, Haydock who left a wife and four children.

YEARSLEY Samuel   aged 26 years.

> A dataller of Earlestown who left a wife and three children.

THE RELIEF FUND.

In those days the relief of the victim's families relied on public subscription and, as there had been several disasters in the district about this time, the difficulties in raising money for yet another were voiced in the press. There had been an explosion at the Hindley Green Colliery, at the Norley Collieries just outside Wigan and at the Rainford Colliery near St. Helens where three men had been killed and four injured.

Richard Evans & Co. provided the families with coffins and a Fund for the Relief of the Victims Dependants was opened with a donation of £800 from the Company. Mr. Legh M.P. and Sir Robert Gerard each donated the sum of £200 and donations came from people of standing in the district and from local firms. The workers of the Haydock Collieries collected £456-6-0d.over two months and the subscription list published in the St. Helens Newspaper dated 2nd. January 1869 shows that a total of £1717-0-0d. had been raised.

At meeting held in Haydock in January, the subscribers expressed a desire that the funds that had been collected for the various disasters should be amalgamated. To this end there was a meeting of the people concerned with the administration of the funds at the Quarter Sessions Court in Wigan. The Mayor of Wigan was in the chair and heard that the Hindley Green Fund stood at £2480 and together with the funds from the Rainford and the Haydock disasters, a considerable sum had been accumulated,

At this meeting it was resolved that the Local Disaster Committees should be instructed to put their funds together and it should be shared for the relief of the families of all the victims of these explosions. It was also resolved that the scales of relief should not exceed in any case the maximum for widows of five shillings a week until death or marriage and for children three shillings a week until the age of fourteen. The Local Committee should look at each individual case and agree the amount of relief with the dependants.

THE INQUEST INTO THE DECEMBER EXPLOSION.

Mr. C. E. Driffield, the County Coroner, arrived in Haydock on Saturday and set up his Court in the Waggon and Horses Hotel in Clipsley Lane. A jury was sworn in and the evidence of identification of the victims was heard. When the Court was satisfied the bodies were released for burial. Most of the funerals took place on the Saturday and the Sunday.

The inquiry into the cause of the explosion that had caused the deaths of the men and boys was opened the following Friday, 8th. January by Mr. Driffield at the Rams Head Hotel, Penny Lane, Haydock. There were several mining experts present. Mr. Peter Higson, Her Majestey's Inspector of Mines. Mr. C. E. Clarke, mining engineer to Sir Robert Gerard of Ashton-in-Makerfield, Mr. Chadwick, the manager of the Haydock Collieries and Mr. William Pickard, the Miners Agent. Mr. Maskell-Peace, solicitor of Wigan, represented Richard Evans & Co.

Proceedings began by examining the evidence of identification of the two victims that had been brought out of the pit alive but had since died from their injuries. Margaret Rogerson, whose husband was a joiner in the village, had assisted in the nursing of Robert Fletcher Room who had lodged with Hugh Arnold and had worked as Arnold's drawer. Room had died from his injuries on January 5th. and Margaret made the official identification to the Court. Room was also known as Robert Fletcher and he is referred to as such in some of the papers of the time. Since he lodged with a family it is likely that he had come to find work from out of the village and, as two christian names were unusual at the time it is very probable that he was known as 'Robert Fletcher'.

Thomas Marsh, brother to Peter, aged eighteen years died on January 1st. Dr. Twyford of St. Helens had attended him but there was little that he could do to save his life.

The Court then got down to the business of determining the cause of the explosion and the first witness to give evidence was Mr. Isaac Billinge, the underlooker of the Wigan Nine Foot Mine and from his first-hand evidence of the explosion we get a clear picture of the conditions that prevailed underground both in the explosion and immediately afterwards.

On the morning of the explosion, he had finished his rounds of inspection and was at home when the browman came to tell him of the disaster at about 12.10 p.m. He went straight to the pit and descended. On reaching the bottom he went to the west side of the workings and very shortly found a pony and two men dead. He heard some moans and went back to get assistance. John Baines and another man came back with him and found Hugh Arnold alive and he was taken out of the mine. Hugh Arnold's account of what happened to him was given at the inquest when he was called as a witness.

Mr. Billinge then went to investigate the west side of the workings in the Ravenhead Mine and found nothing. He returned and helped the men to restore the ventilation in the Wigan Mine and was himself overcome by the afterdamp. He had to be taken from the pit but returned the next morning fully recovered. By then all the bodies had been found and removed with the exception of Thomas Stock. It took a further hour to recover Stock's body.

Mr. Billinge did not know what had caused the explosion but he thought that the combination of gas and gunpowder could have been responsible. A can that had contained powder was found with both the ends blown off in Joseph Marsh's place. The ventilating air went from Joseph Marsh's working place to John Marsh's place where two shots were found. One of these had blown out and the other was partly burnt. This could have been responsible for igniting the gas.

Joseph Greenall, the principle fireman, was found a short distance from these working places and was, in all probability, walking away after making his inspection before the shots were fired. Mr. Billinge stated that Greenall was a very experienced man.

There was a possibility that the gas had been ignited by a faulty lamp and the evidence given by Isaac Billinge gives a very clear account of the system that was used at the colliery to issue lamps. They were given to the men at the pit head and were locked by the banksman before they went into the pit. It was a very serious offence to unlock a lamp in the mine and only the underlooker and the fireman had lamp keys. It was stated that Greenall's lamp was found unlocked but it was the usual practice for the fireman.

Mr. Billinge was then questioned by Mr. Higson, the Government Inspector, about the method of ventilation that was used in the mine. Gas was known to be present in the mine and although the dangers were recognised, it was not considered a major problem provided that the ventilation was good enough to carry the gas away. If the brattice was damaged for any length of time there could be a build up of gas but, as far as was known, all was well in the mine and the fireman had not reported anything dangerous, like damage to the brattice to Mr. Billinge.

Mr. Christopher Fisher Clarke, mining engineer to Sir Robert Gerard of Ashton-in-Makerfield was then called as an expert witness. He had been with the rescue party that had explored the workings after the explosion. His account corroborated what Mr. Billinge had said and he thought that the gas had built up in the workings due to some damaged bratticing. He said that, in his opinion, the mine was safe enough to be worked by candles. In a modern context this may seem very dangerous today, but at the time it was still the practice to use candles or 'open flames' in Lancashire pits and many other mining areas in the country.

Mr. Clarke made the remark to underline his high opinion of the system and the quality of the ventilation in the mine. He was of the opinion that the gas had been ignited when a shot was fired in John Marsh's place and the lesson to be learned for the future was that only the fireman should fire the shots. He concluded his evidence by saying that there was no mismanagement or oversight on the part of either the manager or the underlooker of the mine.

Another expert witness was called, Mr. Samuel Cook, one of the underlookers at Old Boston, another of the Haydock Collieries, who had also taken part in the rescue operations. He gave a graphic account of the conditions and scenes underground in the aftermath of the explosion. He went down the shaft and met some people carrying Hugh Arnold out of the mine. He then went to Mr. Chadwick and they both went down the west side of the workings where they found the body of Peter Simm and a dead pony and discovered the bodies of William Dearden and John Cartwright. He then joined the workers repairing the ventilation and went into he workings on the east side where he found the body of William Pover. He stayed in the mine until eight on Thursday morning and returned at eleven the same day until he came to the surface at four in the afternoon. He told the Court that the men he had found were all burnt and that the greatest signs of burning were in John Marsh's place. The witness could give no explanation as to the cause of the explosion and stated that there was little gas to be found while the rescue operations were going on. The inquest was adjourned until Thursday at ten o'clock and the jury bound over to appear at this time.

The first witness of the second day was Hugh Arnold, the man that the rescuers had found alive and had taken out of the mine. He stated that he was at work on the morning of the explosion when he heard a very loud noise and a strong wind blowing down the tunnel. Realising what had happened and that the situation was dangerous, he left his place very quickly without even picking up his clothes. He had not gone very far when he was overcome by the afterdamp and he remembered nothing of the events of his rescue. He thought that, when he became unconscious, he must have fallen on his lamp since he had a burn on his hip.

He spoke very highly of the fireman, James Greenall, and he told the court that he knew that Greenall inspected his place regularly since there were always chalk marks, in accordance with the General Rules of the Colliery showing that he had been there. On the morning of the explosion, Arnold had seen the deputy fireman, John Merricks, inspect his place and he told the court that he had every confidence in the man's abilities. He had fired a shot that morning and there had been no sign of gas.

The next witness was Joseph Marsh, whose brother John and nephew John jnr. were both killed in the disaster. These were three of the people who had worked at the Pewfall Colliery and had worked for only two or three weeks at the Queen Pit. Joseph did not go to work on the fateful day due to illness and he told the court that his brother was a very experienced miner who could handle explosives well.

In answer to the Coroner's questions, Joseph said that earlier in the week the had had some shots that had misfired and he thought that this was due to the quality of the powder. He saw no danger in the situation since there was no evidence that there was gas present. Mr. Higson, the Inspector, questioned him closely on the arrangements for firing shots in the colliery. Marsh told the court that he fired one shot a day and that he examined his own place before the shot was fired. He did not examine as far as the far end of the workings which were about ten yards away but only the immediate area of his place of work. Mr Higson said, "The whole of the top was really your place and under the Special Rules of the Colliery it was your bounden duty to examine it and it is not asking too much that you should make this inspection when the lives of others were jeopardised thereby". This was an accusation that the man had been negligent.

Marsh again stated that he did not go as far as the end of the workings and the Coroner intervened, "He can not say more Mr. Higson. He should have looked but unfortunately he did not and he was not told by those above him".

Mr. Higson pressed the point but Mr. Pickard and Mr, Driffield again pointed out the Joseph Marsh had not been in-structed by his superiors to search the end of the workings for gas before he fired his shots. At this point Mr Higson let matters rest.

The question as to the use of gunpowder in the mines was a very topical one as there had been two serious explosions in the High Brooks Colliery at Ashton-in-Makerfield a few years earlier which had caused a great loss of life and a gunpowder explosion could have been the cause of the fatalities in this explosion. There was also the question as to how the powder was used in the mine to get coal and this question was to arise later in the inquiry.

Marsh stepped down and Mr. John Chadwick took the stand. He was at Pewfall pit when the explosion occurred and got to Queen Pit between noon and one. He went down the pit and led the exploration. In his opinion the explosion had occurred in John Marsh's place. Marsh had fired a shot about an hour before and, judging by the boxes of coal that he had filled and were standing about sixty yards away, he was ready to fire another shot and had done so.

The brattice in Marsh's place had been pulled down so that it could be moved somewhere else in the mine. This could have led to a build up of gas in the workplace and it was possible that the shot could have ignited it. Another possibility for the presence of the gas was, that there was had been a sudden flow of gas from the coal, called an outburst, but in his opinion, this had not happened.

He went on to say that a few months ago there had been a quantity of gas behind a fault that had exploded and set fire to the coal. Prompted by Mr. Higson, Mr. Chadwick agreed that the method of ventilation could be improved and he outlined his ideas on the subject to the Court.

Mr. Chadwick stepped down and the Court next heard the evidence and comments from Mr. Peter Higson. He had no doubt that there had been a large accumulation of gas in Marsh's place and he thought that the shot had ignited it. The question was, where had the gas come from?

If there had been gas in the other workings then this would have been drawn into the fire and ignited. He thought that this was the case in John Moss's place where charred props were found. He found no evidence of a sudden outburst of gas, but he commented on the way that the ventilation was split and thought that the area of the workings could allow a greater quantity of air to pass through. The Coroner, no doubt mindful of the questioning of Mr. Marsh, specifically asked Mr. Higson if he thought "there was any want of precaution?" Mr. Higson answered the question by general comments on the splitting of the ventilation and the use of brattice in the ventilation system.

After Mr. Higson stepped down, Mr. Driffield summed up the evidence and instructed the jury to retire and consider it's verdict. It took a quarter of an hour and returned the following verdict:-

"That Henry Owen and twenty five certain others came to their deaths by an explosion of firedamp in the Nine Foot Mine, Queen Pit in Haydock on the 30th. December and we find from the evidence before us that the said firedamp was ignited by John Marsh's blown out shot but whether there was a sudden outburst, there was not sufficient evidence to show".

THE AFTERMATH OF THE DECEMBER EXPLOSION.

The inquest verdict closed the affair and the village went on with it's daily life but in the Annual Report of the Inspectors of Mines 1868, Mr. Higson records some further comments on the disaster. He was sure that the gas had been ignited by a blown out shot in Marsh's place and he was critical of the fireman and the use of brattice in the ventilation system.

The fireman, Greenall, who was not named in the Report, was found in a part of the mine where the brattice was supposed to have been down and he had put it back with little thought of the consequences of his actions. As the air flow was restored it would have swept out any gas that had accumulated and he thought it had arrived at Marsh's place just as he fired the shot. in Mr. Higson's opinion the fireman should have found the gas before the ventilation was restored. The gas had accumulated in a working place that had not been used for some time and had not been examined daily by he fireman as was required by the Rules of the Colliery so he was ignorant of it's presence. In the Report he commented:-

"These frequent casualties have disclosed the painful fact that fireman have omitted to make an inspection of places not actually in work, although situated near those workings in which men are daily employed: this shows a serious neglect of duty, into which the owners of the mines should make constant and minute enquiry, and provide a check on their proceedings, whereby neglect or omission may be detected to prevent accidents occurring".

As to the general use of brattice in the ventilation system, Mr. Higson made the following comments:-

"It has recently become the practice to conduct the ventilation of the workings by means of brattice cloth to a considerable extent, on the grounds, no doubt of economy, though some allege, for safety in the event of an explosion taking place, the system cannot be allowed to go on, nor be too soon discontinued. Brattice makes but a delicate and unreliable partition, as it is liable to be broken down by the slightest fall from the roof; it requires constant and unremitted attention on the part of every one in any way connected with the working of the mine, which experience shows is seldom or ever given in the manner and form absolutely required. It did not appear that the underlooker of the mine had inspected the place from which the gas was fired for some time previously, relying on the fireman seeing it was safe. Two days before a collier was sent to make a cut through into a parallel road but he did not go to the end by ten or twelve yards. Neither the underlooker nor the fireman went with this man, who was a stranger to the mine, and ignorant of gas and the mode of dealing with it. He was absent on the day of the explosion and thereby escaped the catastrophe. The owners of the mine would do anything to prevent such a casualty as this and I have always believed that the colliery is well managed. In opening out large areas of new ground, it is a great mistake to conduct the ventilation by means of brattice, except only from one cut through into a parallel road, which should not in any case exceed twenty yards, and in no instance should bratticed places be suspended until they have been opened out at the extreme ends, and communications made with the adjoining places, so that the ventilation may be free of risk. To leave endways or other places depending for their ventilation on brattice is, in all cases, to provide the means of casualty sooner or later, which the facts contained in these pages prove beyond any question or doubt; and such practices will not pass unnoticed".

Mr. Higson's words went unheeded and there were many more deaths in the coalfield as the practice of using brattice continued for many years.

THE EXPLOSION OF 21st. JULY 1869.

Since the December explosion, work had continued at the Queen Pit and the workforce had a generally good opinion of the conditions in the pit and the management of the colliery. It was considered a safe mine, despite the occurrence of the last explosion. Evans & Co. had made important alterations to the system of ventilation of the mine in accordance with the recommendations of the Mines Inspector but the work had not yet been completed. The colliery could have employed about three hundred and fifty men but due to the work on the ventilation system and the general decline in the coal trade, there were seldom above one hundred employed at any one time.

The underground work had been concentrated close to the pit eye and special care had been taken in the the Wigan Nine Foot Mine where the last explosion took place. The work that had been done was carefully planned and inspected but the Inspector of Mines had not been asked to make an inspection since the work was not yet complete.

On Wednesday 21st. July about one hundred men descended the pit. A full inspection of the workings had been made and everything was found to be satisfactory. Work commenced about six a.m. and all went well until five minutes past eleven when the banksman, Thomas Taylor, who was working near the mouth of the shaft saw a momentary reversal of the ventilation and a cloud of dust come from the downcast shaft. He sent someone to look for Mr. Billinge, the underlooker of the mine and repeatedly sent signals to the bottom of the shaft. For several minutes there was no reply and then the cage came to the surface bringing a young man whose name is not recorded, who said that there had

Rescuers Going Down.

been an explosion in the Wigan Nine Foot workings.

Mr. Billinge, who had been down the pit at the time that the explosion occurred, was in the opposite return air course when he was blown off his feet and banged against the wall of the tunnel by the force of the blast. He recovered quickly only too well aware of what had occurred and made his way to the bottom of Legh Pit and from there he hurried the few hundred yards to Queen Pit.

Mr. Chadwick, the underground manager and Mr. Harvey, the Company secretary were quickly at the colliery organising the exploring parties. As news of the accident spread throughout the village, a large crowd of anxious men and women gathered at the pit head. Many were agitated and asked for information as to who was in the mine. Volunteers for the search parties willingly came forward and it was about one p.m. that operations were ready to commence. Up to midnight about sixty men were working in relays and they found that the stoppings were badly damaged, waggons blown to pieces and the first two parties reported that the had found about twenty bodies.

Mr. Harvey and other pit officials set about making arrangements above ground. Twenty three carts were obtained to take the thirty survivors that had been rescued home. Many of these men were in a very bad state suffering from the effects of the afterdamp and some were badly burnt. One of the survivors, William Blinstone, died in the cart on the way home. Drs. Twyford and Jameson from St. Helens arrived at the pit head and tended the survivors. The Reverend Sherlock, the Vicar of Haydock, was also at the scene comforting the anxious crowd.

Mr Richard Evan's sons Joseph and Josiah, were at a meeting in Manchester when the disaster occurred and they were sent a telegram informing them of the event. They were very soon at the colliery. Telegrams were also sent to the Government Inspector of Mines and to Mr. Driffield, the County Coroner. Help also came from the local colliery owners, Mr. Clarke, mining engineer to Sir Robert Gerard of Ashton-in-Makerfield and Mr. J. Stone of Stony Lane Collieries, Hindley, near Wigan, together with Mr. Chadwick supervise the early rescue operations.

One of the rescue parties had a very narrow escape when they were working at the far end of the workings. They came across a large body of afterdamp and first one and then another member of the party collapsed. Mr. Chadwick and Mr. Billinge began to feel the effects of the gas. Billinge went back to get help and Chadwick stayed with the two unconscious men. Mr. Chadwick then began to feel the effects of the gas and decided to go down the tunnel after Mr. Billinge. He saw the glimmer of a lamp in front of him and when he got to the spot he found Billinge unconscious. He went on and very soon found a rescue party who got Billinge and the two men safely out of the pit.

By ten p.m. all the workings had been searched and fifty six bodies recovered. it was after midnight before all the bodies were at the surface, many of them burnt and badly mutilated. They were taken to a shed that had been prepared as a temporary mortuary at the pit head. Here, during the night, they were washed and laid out to await identification. This was a difficult task due to the state of the bodies which indicated the force of the explosion.

During the following morning a constant stream of friends and relatives made their way to the shed to find their loved ones. They had to make their way through a crowd of the curious who peered through the cracks in the shed walls and glanced through the door as it was opened and closed. One man had to visit the place four times before he recognised his son. The floor of the shed was covered with sawdust and disinfectants had to be liberally used, necessary precautions due to the state of the bodies and the hot July weather.

On Thursday, the day after the explosion, Mr. Peter and Mr. John Higson, the Government Inspector and his assistant arrived at the colliery. They, together with Mr. Chadwick and Isaac Billinge descended the pit at about nine a.m. to examine the workings and try to find the cause of the disaster. They were later joined by Mr. Mercer of the Park Lane Collieries, Ashton-in-Makerfield and Mr. Smethurst of the Bryn Collieries also of Ashton. The party came to the surface about noon.

The Nine Foot workings were ventilated by a tunnel, called a jig brow, at the top of which, the air was split and sent east and west. Not many men were working on the east side. The majority of the victims were found on the west side and they had suffered serious burns. There was a tunnel leading from the Nine Foot workings into the Ravenhead Six Foot Mine and some of the victims were found in the latter killed by the afterdamp. In the early editions of the press it was thought that Mr. Higson would make another inspection later in the week. As to the ignition of the gas, it was suspected that gunpowder used in a shot was responsible.

Most of the injured that had been got out of the pit were progressing favourably but some were not. William Yates, the fireman, was said to be the most seriously injured and very badly burnt. A man named Owen was suffering from the effects of afterdamp. William Lucas, aged twelve years, was reported to be in a critical condition suffering from a severely lacerated scalp and a fractured skull and Henry Picton, a dataller of Ashton-in-Makerfield, whose arms, legs and face were badly burnt was also said to be in a critical condition. William Yates and Henry Picton appear on the list of victims but William Lucas, although reported to be so badly injured does not appear on the list and so presumably, survived.

The identification of the dead was a difficult process due to the state of the bodies. One man described as 'hale and hearty' arrived at the shed to protest that a corpse that had been labelled with his name was not in fact him and an accurate identification had to be found for the corpse. The families of two lads could not decide which was which but by Thursday all fifty six victims had been identified. The Wigan Reporter wrote, "There was lamentation, moaning and woe over these fifty six grizzly corpses and too truly did the tears of the women tell the story of the desolate homes which is recorded on the list of the dead".

By Friday the bodies had been placed in coffins to await the inspection of the Coroner's jury which met at the Rams Head Inn, Haydock. On Wednesday 21st. July. Sergeants Gardiner and Murphy of the County Constabulary, the former of Ashton and the latter of Pemberton, Wigan, were in charge of the arrangements at the Coroner's court. Present were Mr. Peter Higson, the Government Inspector for the district, Mr. John Chadwick, the underground manager for Richard Evans & Co., Mr. Isaac Billinge the underlooker of the Haydock Collieries, Mr. Clarke, mining engineer for Sir Robert Gerard, Mr. Mercer of Park Lane Collieries and Mr. William Smethurst of Bryn Collieries all of Ashton-in-Makerfield.

The jury consisted of the foreman, Captain E. Browne, Mr. Joseph Gibbons, Mr. Joseph Radcliffe, Mr. James Cunliffe, Mr. William Finney, Mr. George Hewitt, Mr. James Buckley, Mr. Edward Johnson, Mr. John France, Mr Edward Birchall, Mr. James Clarke, Mr. John Glover and Mr. Edward Edwardson.

Mr. Driffield opened the proceedings with a speech in which he told the jury that it was their sole duty to inquire into the deaths at the colliery. He said that he had no idea as to the cause of the explosion but he had no doubt that the inquiry would ascertain the cause of the disaster.

The first task of the jury was to hear the formal evidence as to the identification of the victims and the first witness was Mr. Thomas Reed of Gibraltar Row, Newton-le-Willows, who was a dataller at the mine. On the morning of the explosion he was at home after after working down the pit until four a.m. He returned to Queen Pit as soon as he heard of the accident and arrived there about noon. He descended the pit to help the rescue parties, which by this time, had found several dead and injured men. The injured were taken out of the pit and Mr. Reed said that one of his sons was among them and was recovering at home slowly. His other son was among those that were killed.

This information is rather confusing since there is no 'Reed' among the list of the dead. However there are only two victims that lived in Gibraltar Row, Newton, Mr. James Billinge, the fireman and John German aged thirteen years. It seems reasonable to assume that the latter was the son of Thomas Reed. Thomas Reed went on to give formal evidence of identification for forty two of the victims.

THE VICTIMS OF THE JULY
EXPLOSION.

BAXENDALE Arnold   aged 20 years.

A drawer of Park Road, Parr who was a single man and was identified by James Fenney who lived in the same road. His body was found in the Six Foot Mine badly burnt and mutilated. He was buried 25th, July at Parr St. Peter's C. of E.

BILLINGE James   aged 44 years.

A fireman of Gibraltar Row, Newton. Married with no family. He was brother to Isaac the underlooker and was identified by Thomas Reed. He was found badly burnt in the Nine Foot Mine.

BLINSTONE William aged 15 years.

Pony driver of Earlestown. He was brought out of the pit alive but died on the cart on his way home. He was identified by his father also named William.

BUNNEY David   aged 13 years.

A pony driver of Havannah, Parr. Identified by Thomas Reed and found burnt in the nine Foot Mine. He was buried at Parr St. Peter's C. of E. 24th, July.

CHADWICK John aged 42 years.

A married collier of Stone Row, Haydock who was found burnt in the Nine Foot mine and identified by Thomas Reed. His son, John was also killed in the explosion.

CHADWICK John aged 13 years.

A drawer of Stone Row, Haydock found burnt in the Nine Foot Mine and identified by Thomas Reed. John was his father and both father and son were buried at Parr St. Peter's C. of E. 24th, July.

CHORLEY John   aged 29 years.

A waggoner of Slater's Yard, Haydock who left a wife and one child. He was found burnt in the Nine Foot Mine. Buried at St. Thomas's C. of E., Ashton-in-Makerfield, 24th. July.

CROSSLEY John   aged 42 years.

A single man, drawer of Twenty Eight Row, Haydock. Found burnt in the Nine Foot Mine and identified by Thomas Reed. He was buried at Parr St. Peter's C. of E. 24th, July where his age is given in the register as 48 years.

DISKIN Patrick   aged 28 years.

A single collier of Unsworth's Cottages, Haydock. Found in the Six Foot Mine, suffocated and identified by Thomas Reed.

DISKIN Thomas   aged 23 years.

A collier of Penny Lane Haydock. Found in the Six Foot Mine suffocated and identified by Thomas Reed.

DEVINE James   aged 16 years.

A pony driver of Haydock Green. James was licensed to Evans & Co. from the Liverpool Reformatory. He was found suffocated in the Six Foot Mine and identified by Thomas McComb.

DUCKWORTH John   aged 15 years.

A drawer of Twenty Eight Row, Haydock, who was single.

DYSON Thomas   aged 15 years.

A pony driver of Stone Row, Haydock. He was found burnt and mutilated in the Ravenhead Mine and was identified by Thomas Reed. He was buried at St. James's C. of E. 25th, July.

EDWARDS Joseph   aged 25 years.

A drawer of Clipsley Lane, Haydock who was single. He was identified by Mary Ann Eden, wife of John Eden of Clipsley Lane. He was found burnt in the Nine Foot Mine.

FAIRCLOUGH Sylvester   aged 40 years.

A tunneller of Wigan who was lodging at New Boston. He left a wife and four children and was found suffocated in the Nine Foot Mine. He was identified by Thomas Reed.

FOLEY John   aged 35 years.

Collier of New Boston, Haydock. He was found suffocated in the Wigan Six Foot Mine and identified by Thomas Reed. He left a wife and four children.

FOSTER Thomas   aged 36 years.

He left a wife and two children. He was a collier and was identified by his wife, Mary Ann who lived in Black brook, Haydock. His body was found in the Six Foot Mine, suffocated.

FINNEY Joseph   aged 32 years.

A collier of Coal Pit Lane, Haydock who left a wife and four children. He was found in the Nine Foot Mine burnt and mutilated and was identified by Thomas Reed who said that Joseph's brother, James was also killed in the explosion.

FINNEY James   aged 20 years.

A single man, collier of Park Road, Parr. He was found burnt in the Nine Foot Mine and was identified by Thomas Reed. Joseph was his brother and they are buried together at St. Peter's C. of E. Parr 25th, July.

GARNETT Thomas   aged 20 years.

A collier of Blackbrook, Haydock who had been married only a few weeks. He was found in the Nine Foot mine burnt and mutilated. He was identified by Thomas Reed. David was his brother.

GARNETT David   aged 32 years.

Collier of Toll Bar, Haydock who left a wife and four children and was found suffocated. He was identified by Thomas Reed. He is buried at St. Peter's C. of E. Parr with his brother Thomas but his mane is given in the burial register as Daniel.

GARRETTY John   aged 38 years.

Collier of Penny Lane, Haydock. he was a widower who left five children. Thomas Reed identified him. He was found suffocated in the Nine Foot Mine.

GERMAN John   aged 13 years.

A taker-off of Gibraltar Row, Newton. He was found in the Nine Foot Mine and was badly burnt and mutilated. He was identified by Thomas Reed and by Mary Smith.

HALL Joseph   aged 16 years.

A drawer of Stone Row, Haydock and the grandson of Abraham Livesley who was also killed in the explosion. He was found in the Six Foot Mine burnt and mutilated and was identified by Thomas Reed.

HALSALL John   aged 51 years.

Collier of Haydock Lane married with three children two of which, James and William were killed in the explo sion. He was found suffocated in the Six Foot Mine and was identified by Thomas Reed.

HALSALL James   aged 13 years.

A drawer of Haydock Lane and the son of John. He was found suffocated in the Six Foot Mine. Identified by Thomas Reed.

HALSALL William   aged 11 years.

Dataller of Haydock Lane. Son of John and brother to James. Found burnt near the pit eye and identified by Thomas Reed. Father and two sons, John. James and William are buried in the same grave at St. Thomas's C. of E., Ashton-in-Makerfield.

HARRISON Richard   aged 41 years.

A collier of Toll Bar, Haydock who left a wife and three children. He was found burnt in the Nine Foot Mine and was identified by Thomas Reed. He was buried 25th, July at Parr St. Peter's.

HATTON James   aged 16 years.

A drawer of Stone Row, Haydock. Brother to William and found suffocated in the Six Foot Mine. Identified by Thomas Reed.

HATTON William   aged 16 years.

A pony driver of Stone Row Haydock, Brother to James and found suffocated in the Six Foot Mine. Identified by Thomas Reed.

HOULTON James   aged 23 years.

A married dataller of Twenty Eight Row, Haydock. Found suffocated in the Six Foot Mine and identified by Thomas Reed.

HOLDING David   aged 17 years.

A labourer of Haydock. He was found in the Nine Foot Mine burnt and mutilated and identified by Abraham Lowe of Ashton who also worked at the colliery.

JOHN Thomas   aged 21 years.

A single drawer who lived at Baines's Row, Haydock. He was found in the Nine Foot Mine burnt and was iden tified by Thomas Reed.

LIVESLEY Abraham   aged 59 years.

A collier of Stone Row, Haydock. He left a wife and eight grown up children. One of his grandsons, Joseph Hall, was also killed in the explosion. He was found suffocated in the Six Foot Mine and was identified by Thomas Reed.

LOWE John   aged 14 years.

A dataller of Town Green Ashton. He was found near the pit-eye and was identified by Thomas Reed.

MOLYNEAU Edward   aged 11 years.

A pony driver of Blackbrook, Haydock who was identified by Elizabeth Marsh of New Boston, Haydock who was his mother. He was found in the Nine Foot Mine burnt and mutilated.

MOLYNEAU Thomas   aged 50 years

A collier of Park Road, Parr. a widower with two children. He was the father of Thomas aged 15 years and identified by Thomas Reed. Both father and son are buried at Parr St. Peter's C. of E. 25th, July.

MOLYNEAU Thomas   aged 15 years.

A pony driver of Park Road, Parr, son of Thomas. He was found in the Nine Foot Mine, burnt and was identified by Thomas Reed. He was buried at St. Peter's C. of E. Parr 25th, July.

MOORE William   aged 45 years.

A collier of Twenty Eight Row, Haydock who left a wife and one child.

MORGAN James   aged 25 years.

A single man who worked as a tunneller and lived in Barnes Row, Haydock. He was found in the Nine Foot Mine, suffocated and was identified by Thomas Reed. He was buried at Parr St. Peter's C. of E. 25th, July.

OWEN James   aged 20 years.

A single collier of Clipsley Row, Haydock who was identified by Mary Ann Smith as her husband's drawer and her cousin. He was found suffocated in the Six Foot Mine.

PARR Thomas   aged 16 years.

A pony driver of Toll Bar, Haydock. He was brother to Henry and was found suffocated in the Six Foot Mine. he was identified by Thomas McComb.

PARR Henry   aged 12 years.

A drawer of Toll Bar, Haydock and was identified by Aaron Livesley of Stone Row, Haydock who was an engine tenter. He was buried with his brother at St. Thomas's C. of E. Ashton 25th. July.

PARFETT Joseph   aged 25 years.

A collier who left a wife and two children. He was found burnt in the Six Foot Mine and identified by Esther Evans with whom he lodged. He was buried at St. James's C. of E., Haydock 25th. July.

PICTON Henry   aged 29 years.

A dataller of Newton Heath. He was found in the Nine Foot Mine badly burnt but he was brought out of the pit alive. He died on the Sunday after the explosion. He was identified by his brother, Thomas a hingemaker of Ashton-in-Makerfield.

PILKINGTON James   aged 36 years.

A collier of Coal Pit Lane, Haydock who left a wife and six children all under the age of eight. He was found in the Nine Foot Mine and was identified by Thomas Reed.

RENDER John   aged 27 years

A tunneller with two children of Spring Terrace, Haydock. He was fond in the six Foot Mine and identi fied by Esther Lightfoot with whom he lodged.

ROSCOE Peter   aged 32 years.

A collier of Toll Bar Haydock who left a wife and four children. He was found in the Six Foot Mine, suffocated and was identified by Thomas Reed. He was buried at St. Peter's C. of E. Parr 25th, July.

RUSSELL Thomas   aged 30 years.

A collier of Toll Bar, Haydock with two children who was found burnt and mutilated in the Nine Foot Mine.

SEDDON Thomas   aged 45 years.

A collier of New Boston, Haydock who left a wife and three children. He was found in the Six Foot Mine and was identified by Thomas Lee with whom he was working at the time of the explosion.

SMITH Henry   aged 26 years.

He left a widow and two children. A collier of Park Road, Parr who was identified by Thomas Reed. He was buried at St. Peter's C of E Parr 25th July.

SOUTHERN Mathew   aged 41 years.

A collier of Clipsley row, Haydock, married with seven children. Robert was one of those children. he was found in the Six Foot Mine, suffocated and identified by Thomas Reed.

SOUTHERN Robert   aged 18 years.

A dataller of Clipsley Row, Haydock, son of Mathew. he was found in the Six Foot Mine, suffocated and identified by Thomas Reed.

TOPPING John   aged 53 years.

A tunneller of Chapel Lane, Wigan who was lodging in New Boston, Haydock. He was a widower with two children and was found suffocated in the Nine Foot Mine. Identified by Thomas Reed.

WESTHEAD James   aged 11 years.

A pony driver of Twenty Eight Row, Haydock who was found burnt in the Nine Foot Mine. He was identified by his brother, William.

WILCOCK Ralph   aged 25 years.

A collier of Haydock. A single man who was found suffocated in the Six foot Mine and identified by Thomas Reed. Buried at St. Thomas's C. of E., Ashton, 24th July.

WINSTANLEY William aged 42 years.

A collier of Twenty Eight Row, Haydock who left a wife and three children. he was found in the Nine Foot Mine burnt and mutilated and was identified by Thomas Reed. He was buried at Parr St. Peter's C. of E. 24th, July.

YATES William.

A fireman of Haydock. He was rescued from the mine and was badly burnt and injured. He was identified by Jane Prescott of Spring Terrace, Haydock. She said that she had heard him ask where the gas had fired and it was her opinion that he did not know.

According to the local papers of the time the list of fifty nine men and boys includes two that were not in fact dead. One collier was reported to have left the pit "in some distress" and ran all the way home clothed only in his shirt. His name is not recorded. Later he sent his sister to the colliery to say that he had survived.

Another collier is reported to have arrived at the mortuary, "hale and hearty" to say that the body that had been identified as his was not in fact him.

This would give a total number of victims of fifty seven, a figure that is referred to in the papers but Mr. Higson, in the Inspectors Report of 1869 refers to the fifty nine victims. Unfortunately they are not listed by name in the Report of the Mines Inspector as they were in later years. The list above includes the fifty nine names that were undoubtly lost their lives in the Queen Pit explosion.

THE FUNERALS OF THE VICTIMS OF THE JULY EXPLOSION.

The funerals were solemn affairs. In the village of Haydock, miner's houses fronted the main roads and had well tended gardens. Waving wheat reached almost to the back doors and all too many of the cottages had their blinds drawn as a mark of respect for the dead. The funeral of James Devine, the boy from the Liverpool Reformatory Association who had been placed in the charge of Richard Evans & Co., was accompanied by a large number of boys from the Institution in Liverpool. It was believed that his mother was in the Liverpool Workhouse and the boy had been sent to the Reformatory for some small misdemeanour. The Reverend Sherlock, the vicar of Haydock, conducted the service at St. James church for him and four Haydock colliers. There were sixteen choristers and he preached from Luke xvi,v 31 "If they do not hear Moses and the prophets neither will they be persuaded, though one rose form the dead".

The funerals of several men took place at St. Peter's C. of E., Parr on Saturday evening and were conducted by the Reverend A.A.Nunn. It was a very quiet affair with the coffins arriving at the church either singly or in pairs and as each arrived the funeral service was read. Hundreds of people, many of them colliers, followed the coffins. A father and his son were among he victims. The father, John Chadwick, was described as "a respectable, well conducted man who was determined to train his family in the paths of virtue and religion". His son, also named John, regularly went to the Sunday School and to mark their respect for the lad, several members of the Sunday School attended the funeral and after the coffin was placed on the hearse they sang a hymn that moved the onlookers to tears.

One funeral followed another. In each ease the principle relatives were in the mourning coaches and some mourners followed on foot. They passed through a large silent crowd, silent as a mark of respect. Throughout the district, crowds of sympathetic women gathered in front of the houses of the bereaved to offer sympathy and consolation.

RELIEF EFFORTS FOR THE VICTIMS DEPENDANTS.

Financial relief for the dependants of the victims was needed quickly as so many of the families had lost their bread winners. The coffins were provided by Richard Evans & Co. They were of oak and had a brass plate on which was engraved the victims name, age and the date of his death. The Colliery Sick Fund provided immediate payments to the families, eight pounds being paid for an adult victim and four pounds for a lad that was lost. Funds were raised all over the district and the Reverend W. A. Mocatta M.A., the Vicar of St. Thomas's, Eccleston, near St. Helens had a special collection at a service that filled the church. The congregation was attended by the local Loyal Order of Orangemen and the church was filled to capacity. Twenty pounds was raised towards the disaster fund.

With the collections that had been made for the December explosion and the other disasters in the district, the fund stood at seven thousand pounds and the trustees found it possible to pay the widows five shillings a week with an extra three shillings for every child that was not at work. It was reported, "that some families got as much as seventeen shillings a week from the fund but further subscriptions were required".

With the funerals over, the Coroner's Court then met to establish the cause of the explosion that had caused the deaths of the fifty nine victims.

THE INQUEST INTO THE JULY EXPLOSION.

The inquest that took place after the second explosion was resumed on Wednesday 27th, July at the Rams Head Inn, Haydock. It was not the usual affair that took place after a mining accident. There was too much to explain with the second explosion taking place in the same mine so soon after the first.

The gentlemen present in court on that first day were, Mr. P Higson, Inspector of Mines for the area, Mr Maskell-Peace, solicitor of Wigan who represented Richard Evans & Co., Mr. Mercer of Mercer and Evans, Park Lane Collieries, Ashton-in-Makerfield, Mr. Clarke, mining engineer to Sir Robert Gerard, Mr. Glover, surveyor to Mr. W. J. Legh M.P., the Reverend Sherlock, vicar of Haydock and the Revered H. Newsham, Roman Catholic priest of Ashton-in-Makerfield.

The form of the inquest was similar with the men giving evidence and then expert witnesses being called but running throughout the proceedings there was a tension that surfaced many times in the court sessions and if we read between the lines of the sources that are available, there were very strong feelings in the village, may of them brought about by a community being in deep shock after being visited by two disasters in such a short time. There also emerges a clear picture of mining practices at the time and the tensions that drove on the exploitation of the rich coal seams of Lancashire.

Mr. Peace opened the proceedings by stating, on behalf of the owners and the proprietors, that they were very anxious that the fullest investigation as to the cause of the explosion should take place and that their sole desire was that everything that could be done for the safety of the workforce in the mine would be done.

Mr Isaac Billinge was the first witness to be called. The underlooker of the Haydock Collieries gave a brief description of the two mines and presented a plan of the workings to the court that showed the ventilation system that was employed in them before the explosion. He thought that the explosion had occurred in James Pilkington's brow. He said that locked lamps were used in the mine. They were locked by the banksman at the surface and inspected underground by the fireman, William Yates. William Yates was the senior fireman and James Billinge, Isaac's brother, was the junior fireman and shotlighter.

When questioned by Mr. Higson, Isaac Billinge gave details of the flow of air through the workings. He thought that there had been a fall of roof prior to the explosion that had interrupted the ventilation. This would allow the gas to accumulate and he thought that it could have been ignited by a shot. He did not think that his brother or William Yates had fired the shot since they were found a considerable distance from Pilkington's place. He had inspected the workings the day before and had found nothing that caused him any concern.

The foreman of the jury asked Mr. Billinge about the use and storage of powder in the mine and it transpired that the colliers provided their own powder and, within the Rules of the Colliery, there was no restriction on how much they used or how often they used it. There was no way of knowing how much powder there was in the mine at the time of the explosion but a little time before twenty five pounds had been used to blast through some rock. Mr Billinge thought that powder had something to do with the explosion but he thought that there was also gas present.

The presence of gunpowder in the mine was an important point that would be the source of much questioning and investigation during the inquiry. Gunpowder was the only explosive that was available at the time and there had been many accidents with it's use in mines. Loss of life had occurred at the Park Lane collieries in Ashton-in-Makerfield a few years before and the Inspector had found the gunpowder was the cause of the explosions and it would be in everybody mind that powder could have something to do with this explosion. We shall see late that another Mines Inspector, Mr. Joseph Dickenson had very strong feelings on the use of powder in the mines.

Mr. Billinge stepped down and the next witness was Joseph Wright, of Coal Pit Lane, Haydock, a collier who had worked in the Nine Foot Mine for about five months and had left the colliery about a month before the explosion to earn more money. He told the court that the victims James and Joseph Finney were related to him and when he worked at the colliery, Joseph and he worked at the front of the brow and Smith and Pilkington worked at the back of the brow. He said that he had encountered gas on only one occasion and that was because the brattice had not been placed close enough to the coalface. He stated that when shots were fired, the fireman always examined the place and he had never known a shot to be fired without this inspection. The sole reason that he had left the pit was to earn more money and he was perfectly satisfied with the work of the officials and the way in which the mine was run.

When he was questioned by a juryman about the amount of gunpowder that he would use, he said that he frequently took five or six pounds down the mine in a day and used it all. He was closely questioned by Mr. Higson and Mr. Pickard, the miners agent, about the presence of gas in the mine and he said that he was perfectly satisfied with the quality of the stoppings and the ventilation system. He once saw a blower that was alight and he put it out with his shirt. He told the fireman and they were both of the opinion that there was no need for alarm since there was enough ventilation to dilute the gas.

James Finney of Park Road, Parr was the next witness. He had worked in the Nine Foot Mine for about three months and had left the colliery about six weeks before the disaster in which he lost two sons. He told the court how he left the colliery. He had used the excuse that the underlooker would not change his place of work so he could leave the job without giving notice. He said that the real reason for leaving was that he had been told to fill in a place with dirt. He knew of several places in the mine where this had been done and, in his opinion, it was dangerous practice since gas could collect in these places. Mr. Finney said that in his fifty years experience as a collier he thought that the management was wrong to allow holes to be filled with dirt and he thought that this was a dangerous practice as the holes were poorly constructed. He had related his fears to his sons but they had decided to stay at work in the mine.

He had never seen gas in the mine and thought that the ventilation was good and all the workforce worked with locked lamps that were provided by the owners. Mr. Finney stated that he took only the powder that he would need for the day down the mine. This amounted to five or six pounds but he knew men that worked near him sometimes take ten or eleven pounds down the pit. When questioned by Mr. Higson he expressed the opinion that it was a hard mine to work and could not be worked at all without the use of powder.

An Awkward Passage.

The foreman of the jury questioned Mr. Finney about the possibility that colliers smoked and drank alcohol in the pit. This may seem a little strange but it was not an unusual question as many of the mines in the locality at this time permitted smoking down the pit, particularly in the St. Helens area and many a collier arrived for work showing signs of a good time the night before. Mr. Finney replied that although he smoked at home, he never smoked in the pit and said that he would have reported anyone he found smoking in the pit to the fireman but he hinted that there were some in the pit who would turn a blind eye to smoking underground.

As to alcohol he had never seen anyone drunk underground but he admitted that it was possible to take drink down the pit as the colliers drinks were not inspected at the surface. However if anyone arrived for work at the colliery drunk, the banksman would not let them down the pit. The Government Inspector commented that he believed that half the explosions that had occurred in the district were due to men drinking overnight and being unequal to their work the following morning. Mr. Finney replied that he did not think a man could do his work if he took a pint of beer below ground.

Thomas Reed, who identified so many of the victims at the first sitting of the court was then recalled to give evidence. He had worked in the mine for about four months as a dataller, working on the ventilation system at night. The coalmining operations took place during the day. When he came up the pit at four a.m. on the morning of the explosion, he had been working on the jig brows and had seen no gas or any falls of roof. It was the duty of the fireman, James Billinge, to inspect all the workplaces before the workforce came down the pit. This was the main job of the fireman in any mine and the job specification was laid down in the Special

Rules of the Colliery. The workforce in any mine had to have full confidence in the firemen as their lives depended on this key official. Mr. Reed saw Mr. Billinge going down the pit as he came up and he had never known him not to inspect all the workplaces before the men arrived every morning. He said that he had not seen gas in the mine for about two months and on that occasion it had been dispersed satisfactorily. Never, to his knowledge, had a shot been fired without the presence of the fireman and the places where the bodies of James Billinge and several others were found, near a ventilation door, was a place where they regularly took cover when a shot was fired.

He thought that the coal could have been got without the use of powder but this would have been more expensive to the owners and the men preferred to use powder in the mine. He confirmed the previous evidence as to the system of lamps used in the mine but he was critical of the ventilation system that allowed air from the Nine Foot Mine to be sent directly into the Six Foot Mine.

John Worsick, of Ashton, also a dataller, at the colliery and had been down the pit the night before the explosion was the next to give evidence and he verified all the Thomas Reed had said to the court.

Up to now, relatively few of the workforce had come forward to give evidence to the Court and as the proceedings for the day were coming to a close and arrangements were being made as to who was to give evidence the following day when Mr. Peace made the comment to the court that at a Miners' Conference in Manchester a few days before, Mr. William Pickard, the miners agent, had said something to the effect that some of the men were afraid to come forward and give evidence. He went on to say that the colliery proprietors were most anxious to find the cause of the disaster and that if anyone wished to give evidence, they could be sure that there would be no reprisals against them from the Company. The foreman of the jury said that it would be more satisfactory if more witnesses came forward and Mr. Peace again reiterated that there would be no action against a witness whether they were employed by the company or not. There was obviously some reason why the workforce felt a reluctance to come forward and give evidence. Exactly what it was would unfold at later sessions of the Court. At this point the proceedings were adjourned until ten the following morning.

At the resumption of the inquest, the same gentlemen were present together with Mr. Josiah Evans and Mr. William Smethurst of the Bryn Collieries, Ashton-in-Makerfield. the list of jurors was called and the Coroner addressed them saying that there was little evidence offered from working miners. The fireman, William Yates, was still too ill to appear in court and he would be a key witness. A juryman suggested that the statement of the proprietors should be repeated to each witness and the Coroner commented that what had been said in court the day before would now be fully known to all the men. Mr. Peace, on behalf of the proprietors, repeated the statement that he had made the day before, that any person who knew anything about the explosion or the system of management should come forward and state it and he assured the court that Richard Evans & Co. would do all that the could to clear up the matter.

The Coroner told the court that when he had been standing in the graveyard on Sunday at the funerals of some of the men, he had heard a man talking about gas in the mine but the man would not tell him who had told him about the gas. At the time the Police sergeant was standing with him. He went on to say that he did not believe that the Company would allow their workforce into a mine that they knew was dangerous.

James Marsh, a collier of Clipsley Cottages, was the next to be called. He had worked at the Queen Pit but now worked at Legh Pit and he was in the mine at the time of the explosion, employed in driving a tunnel or brow. He said that he had often found gas when he came to work and on occasions he had been allowed to work in gas. The gas cleared after about half an hour because the brattice was well placed and sometimes, he cleared the gas out of the place by sweeping it with his jacket. This was common practice at the time, called "brushing out the gas" and was often used by colliers in local mines. Since he had been working in the brows he had seen little gas and when he did, the firemen had been informed and chalked "FIRE" on a spade which was the procedure that was laid down in the Rules of the Colliery. The place was always inspected by the fireman. Although he was down the pit at the time of the explosion he knew of it only because the officials told him.

The Coroner asked him directly if he thought that there was anything wrong with the management of the mine to which Mr. Marsh replied, "No. I don't think there is. It has been as well managed as any mine that I have worked in. The firemen were attentive to their duties and the places well bratticed".

He was then questioned by Mr. Higson about the occasions on which he had found gas in the workings and he said that the flame in his lamp had indicated the presence of gas and although it was sometimes ten yards thick and a yard deep, he had dealt with it himself. He now thought that he should have reported it to the firemen. When he did so they allowed him to go on working but they moved the "FIRE" notice further down the workings. The firemen at the time was John Mercer, who was now dead, he was killed in the December explosion and John Millington who was still employed at Legh pit. He told the court that he remembered a man called John Harrison remarking on the presence of gas about a week before the explosion. The Coroner asked Mr. Billinge if Harrison was still employed at the colliery and was told that he was and that his evidence would be obtained.

Mr. Pickard then questioned the witness who said that the ventilation was taken to the face by bratticing but the gas sometimes accumulated. He said that the Special Rules of the Colliery prohibited men working in gas and that it was the responsibility of the firemen to clear the gas. He agreed with Mr. Pickard that men should not work in these conditions. Mr. Peace took up the cross examination and asked,

"But you thought that you could sweep the gas out as well as anyone else?"

"Yes".

"Did you feel any danger from it?"

"No."

The foreman asked if the regulations for firing shots in the mine were being observed and Mr. Marsh told the court that the fireman was always present when shots were fired and that the regulations were strictly observed.

The reason why the men were reluctant to come forward and give evidence again surfaced when Mr. Pickard questioned the witness about the rumours that the men were afraid of reprisals from the Company if they came forward to give evidence. James Marsh answered that he knew of no one that had been sacked because they had given evidence to the inquiry into the December explosion. He could not speak for others but he had no hesitation in coming forward to give evidence and he had never heard of anyone who said that they were afraid to do so. Mr. Pickard said that he had heard of a man named Hugh Arnold who was a survivor of the December explosion loosing his job at the colliery. Mr.

Peace confirmed that the man had given evidence to the December inquiry and Mr. Pickard went on to say that he man had lost his job at the colliery. There were rumours that Arnold had made false claims on the Colliery Club, a kind of early provident society, and this was the reason that he was discharged. Mr. Driffield interceded that Mr. Billinge would know the circumstances under which Arnold lost his job and Mr. Billinge was recalled.

He said, that as far as he knew, Arnold was discharged for making undue claims on the Club and for taking away timber from the colliery to make a sofa. He was caught red handed and left the colliery in May. Mr. Billinge was interrupted by the Coroner who said that no further particulars were required but it was better that the matter raised by Mr. Pickard, were settled and the sooner the better.

Mr. Pickard was not satisfied and said that on the day of the July explosion, Arnold had told him that he did not know why he was discharged. The Coroner put forward the view that perhaps he did not want to disclose the reason for his dismissal to Mr. Pickard and at this point the matter was left but it was to come to the attention of the Court later.

The foreman of the jury then raised a serious point which caused a minor crisis in the Court and tried the patience of the Coroner. He said, "A juryman tells that one of the witnesses called yesterday has stated to him that he did not speak the truth."
"What witness is that?" asked the Coroner.
"Joseph Wright", replied the juryman.
"He told me the same ", said another juryman.
The Coroner asked Sergeant Gardiner who was the local Police officer from the County Constabulary, if Wright was in court and the Sergeant replied that he was not.

"It seems rather a strange thing, that a juryman should have been in conversation with a witness after our meeting here", said the Coroner, "It occurs to me, that if we are taking notice of what is said by a man, who, after being sworn to tell the truth, the whole truth and nothing but the truth we shall have our work cut out".

"I do not think it matters much if we can only get at the truth", said the foreman.

"I do not use the word truth in the sense you mean Mr. Foreman. It seems to me arrant nonsense to take here what is said on oath and then to listen to what is said afterwards".

"But if the man dare not tell the truth ————".

"Then he has committed perjury", said Mr. Driffield, "It either amounts to that or it is all nonsense. The man has sworn to tell the truth, the whole truth, and nothing but the truth and then he goes away and says he has not told the truth".

"He has not told us all he knows", a juryman said.

"Then he can not avoid having committed perjury".

Mr. Higson entered the discussion to try to defuse an awkward situation, "Unless he came forward and said that he had forgotten to tell us something".

"That is a different thing", said Mr. Driffield, "If such is the case, he is quite at liberty to come forward".

The foreman of the jury said that he thought it was their duty to look into the matter and the Coroner read over Wright's evidence. Mr. Peace pointed out that the witness was not employed by Evans & Co.

"Do you think it to be an idle story and we ought to pass it over?", asked the foreman.

"I think so, " replied the Coroner, "In as much as the only case to have him brought here in the charge of an officer and ask him if he has committed perjury. and then which statement do we trust?"

"Well I think it ought to be done", said the foreman.

"I prefer not to do it. Could a man speak more in favour of the proprietors that he did yesterday?"

"But he has told this to two jurymen".

"Never mind what he said. The pity is that the jury permit themselves to hear what is said under these circumstances".

Mr. Peace said, "It would be more satisfactory to the proprietors of the colliery, if the man could be sent for and asked to explain what he means by this statement".

"I prefer not to recognise any such fact," said the Coroner, "He has already sworn before the jury that he knows nothing wrong".

"And perhaps he will do it again," said a juror.

"I infer that he would," said Mr. Driffield, "We have nothing to do with the statement outside". And there the matter was laid to rest.

Mr. William Boarden of Heyes Green, Haydock was the next witness and the Coroner reminded him of the proprietor's statement before he was sworn in. Mr. Boarden then gave his evidence. He was a labourer in the Six Foot Mine at Queen Pit and was underground at the time of the explosion. He related how he was with four other men when he felt a wind and, knowing what had happened, they made their way down the brow behind an empty box using it to push open a ventilation door. He was then overcome by afterdamp and could not remember passing through a second door or how he got out of the pit. One of the three men with him was found dead where they left the box and another was found dead in the roadway to the pit eye. He testified that the ventilation was good and that he had never seen gas in the mine.

The next witness was John Harrison of Haydock, whose name had been mentioned in Court before. He had worked in the Nine Foot Mine for about ten months as a dataller. One night about two weeks before the explosion, he was working with Henry Picton, one of the deceased, when they found gas in a newly started tunnel. There was a large quantity of gas and they reported it to the underlooker who commented that it was strange. The tunnel was level, about five yards long and well bratticed. He said that the ventilation was good and that he thought the fireman, James Billinge did his duty well.

William Smith, a collier of Gibraltar Row, who was in the mine at the time of the explosion and was affected by the after-damp said that he had never seen gas in the mine for the three or four years that he had worked there. He was critical of the ventilation system of the mine that took the air from one mine to another and he believed that the men in the Main Delf would not have been killed if the air crossing had not been damaged in the explosion.

John Barnes, of Old Fold, Haydock, was in the Six Foot Mine at the time of the explosion and he was the next to give his evidence. He was affected by the afterdamp but managed to get out of the pit. He had seen little gas in the pit and he thought the ventilation and the management good and the firemen very attentive to their duties.

Mr. William Wood, of Park Road, Parr was a collier in the Six Foot Mine and was affected by afterdamp before he could get out of the pit. He had found gas in his place a few days before the explosion but the fireman had left the usual signal. He had also worked in the Nine Foot Mine and he said that compared to this, his place in the Six Foot was a little hot but there was always plenty of air. He stated that powder was not used in the Six Foot and that if it was he would not have liked to have worked there. Questioned by Mr. Pickard, he said that he thought Pilkington to be a steady man who would not fire a shot before the fireman had made an inspection of the place. The fireman was a very efficient man and

John Mercer was the first expert witness to be called. He had been a mining engineer but was now the principle partner of Mercer and Evans of Park Lane Collieries, Ashton-in-Makerfield. He stated that he was at the colliery after the explosion and had inspected the workings. Since then he had made two further inspections of the mine. He told the court that he thought the gas could have come from a large fall about half way up Pilkington's brow. There had been a previous fall there and the place was well timbered but the new fall had brought this down. The fall was a new one since the rails on either side of it had been torn up by the force of the explosion. He thought that the gas had come from this fall and travelled up the brows worked by Pilkington and Finney. A lamp had been found in Finney's brow by Mr. Clarke that had a damaged gauze. He thought it had been holed by a pick and in this state it could have ignited any gas that was present. He also thought that there had been a second explosion in the two other adjoining brows. He had noted that several powder cans had exploded which could account for the second explosion. In his opinion the ventilation of the mine was good and he did not consider it to be a fiery mine.

Proceedings for the day were drawing to a close when Mr Driffield told the court that at the next sitting Mr. Joseph Dickenson the Government Inspector of Mines for the Manchester area would be present. This was unusual, two Government Inspectors appearing at the same inquiry but the jury had requested him to be present which underlined the importance of the proceedings.

At this point the Coroner was then asked by Mr. Pickard if he would be called as a witness as he was representing the interests of the miners. The foreman said that this was a good idea. Mr. Higson asked if Mr. Evans had any objection and he said that he did not. Mr. Evans said that he had had a conversation with Mr.

Pickard after Mr. Pickard had inspected the workings and declared himself satisfied. At this point Mr. Pickard got to his feet and the tensions of the court room again emerged.

"Oh, no Sir. You are mistaken", said Mr. Pickard.

"That is what I understand you told Mr. Billinge, the person to which you spoke of it", replied Mr. Evans.

"That is so", said Mr. Billinge.

Mr. Evans continued, "And I notice that, at a meeting in Manchester this week, Mr. Pickard made a speech which is at variance with what he said in Haydock last January. He is quite at liberty to go down the mine."

"I wish to put myself right in this matter," said Mr. Pickard, "I did not express myself at the last inquiry, satisfied with the workings. I said to Mr. Billinge that I was satisfied with the conduct of the firm in allowing me to go down and make an examination. That was my meaning. I did not refer to the state of the workings".

The Coroner asked Mr. Evans if he would allow Mr. Pickard to inspect the workings and Mr. Evans agreed. At this point the court was adjourned until the next Tuesday.

The fourth sitting took place on Tuesday 3rd. August and the court heard the news that the fireman, William Yates, had died from his injuries on Wednesday without saying anything about the explosion. This was a great loss as he was a key eyewitness and brought the total death toll to fifty nine men and boys. The hearing was attended by the same gentleman and Mr. Joseph Dickenson, the Government Inspector from the Manchester Area who was there at the invitation of the jury.

The first witness was Mr. James Finney of Park Road, Parr who had worked in the Nine Foot Mine up to three months before the explosion. he stated that he had left the colliery to earn more money and for no other reason. This was a point that was to reappear in the evidence given by the men. The coal in the mine was very hard and could only be got with the use of gunpowder. As the colliers were paid for the coal that they won, it was easier for them to make a living in another mine and as we shall see many of them left Queen pit for just this reason.

Mr. Finney said he could find no fault with the mine. About three weeks before he had left, his workmate had hurt himself and he was unable to carry on the work on his own. Mr. James Billinge had offered to take him round the mine and show him the places where there was gas. About one hundred yards up an old brow, there had been a fall that had been well timbered when it was repaired. Mr. Billinge lifted his lamp and the flame indicated the presence of gas. The witness went on to say that they went round the whole of the Nine Foot Mine, including the site of the December explosion but it was only in the one place described that they detected any gas.

Mr. Higson asked the witness if there was anyone working in the place at the time and Mr. Finney said that there was not and that the ventilation was good.

The foreman asked about the amount of powder that was taken down the mine and Finney said that he took down about five or six pounds a day which was the amount that he would use in a days work. The foreman then asked him if he thought it was wise to wall off a tunnel that was known to contain gas. The Coroner interjected that this was a question for a mining engineer but the foreman said that a man who had some forty years mining experience should know something of the matter. Mr. Finney said that he was a collier and could answer the question as well as anyone else. He thought that the gas would all turn to blackdamp and not seep out. The colliers of the time thought that this is what would happen to the gas but we know now that they were mistaken and, in retrospect, we can see that the Coroner's remarks were fully justified. Mr. Higson asked about the bratticing and he said that he knew it was wrong to work with bratticing so far but he thought it a matter for Mr. Chadwick, the General Manager of the Haydock Collieries.

James Harrison, of Park Road, Parr was the next witness. Up to a month before the explosion, he was a collier in the nine Foot Mine and had left to earn more money. He had worked with Joseph Parfett. David and Thomas Garnett worked behind them. They were all victims of the explosion. He had worked there for almost six months and had never seen any gas but he had heard some men talk of gas in the old brows. He said that he always fired his own shots but only after a fireman's inspection. On some occasions this had taken place while he was ramming the shots home and on these occasions he had always made a careful inspection of the place himself before firing the shots. He was asked by the Coroner if he has any objection to the mine at all and it transpired that he did not like the far end of the workings and stated that if he was asked to work there he would have left the colliery since the air in that place was sometimes warm. He had heard some of the men saying that they did not like the mine, not because of the danger of gas but because the coal was hard and difficult to get and it took a great deal of powder which the men had to provide for themselves. this was why he had left and he thought he could earn more money in another colliery.

When questioned by the fireman, Mr. Harrison said that the underlooker used to visit the mine about once a week but he had seen Mr. Chadwick only once in the time that he worked at the colliery. Mr. Peace was quick to point out that besides the inspections by Mr. Isaac Billinge, the underlooker, there were also daily inspections by the two firemen, James Billinge and William Yates. The witness stepped down.

Next on the stand was Joseph Webster of Haydock, a collier, who had worked in the Nine Foot Mine up to three weeks before the explosion but had left to earn more money as the coal was hard at Queen Pit. The mine was satisfactory as far as he was concerned. He said that he used to prepare three shots at a time with about one and a half pounds in each charge. The fireman always examined the place before the shots were fired and stayed until the fuse was lit.

Hugh Arnold, the survivor of the December explosion, whose name had been mentioned in court at a previous hearing was the next to address the court and to give his explanation of the events leading to his dismissal from the colliery. He handed the Coroner a copy of the Wigan Observer in which it stated the Mr. Billinge has said that he was dismissed from the colliery for an imposition on the Colliery Club and for taking timber away from the colliery for his own use.

Mr. Billinge spoke, "That was wrong and I will put it right".

Several jurymen pointed out that it had been said.

"It was a mistake", said Mr. Billinge, "What I meant to have said was that he made a sofa or something out of the timber that had been sent to the house ———".

"It never belonged to the colliery. It was my own," interrupted Mr. Arnold

Mr. Billinge said that it had been acknowledged that it had been sent to the house

The Coroner asked, "What did you leave the colliery for, Arnold?"

"I never knew".

"And you told me so on the night of the explosion," said Mr. Pickard.

The foreman said, "There is no doubt that the man was accused of thieving before us".

"It was my mistake," said Mr. Billinge.

"For what was the man discharged?" asked the Coroner.

"I know nothing further about it. He had nothing to do with me", said Mr. Billinge.

"Who discharged him?" asked the Coroner.

"I do not know".

The Coroner asked Arnold if he gave evidence at the inquest into the December explosion.

"Yes. I was the only one brought out of the Nine Foot workings alive at the last explosion".

"Do you think that they gave you your discharge because you were playing instead of working?" asked the Coroner.

"I was ill, Sir. My Club money was refused".

"Was there some difficulty about the Club?" asked Mr. Peace, "Some question as to your getting your wages when you were getting relief?"

"Not that I know of", replied Arnold.

Mr. Chadwick, the General Manager of the Haydock Collieries then spoke.

"The only reason for his discharge that I ever heard was that it was of something in connection with the Club".

"What do you think you were discharged for?" the Coroner asked.

"I do not know, sir".

"And you want it explaining?"

"I should like it to be explained".

"If the Coroner will allow me. I think I can explain the matter", said Mr. Josiah Evans, "After the last explosion, Arnold was taken on at Parr, and after working there a short time, he again declared for the Club from which he expected to obtain six months pay. The visitors among the workmen refused to take him on the Club, and we, seeing that he was imposing on the Club, refused to allow him to work again. That is the reason why he was discharged".

-69-

"Was he discharged on regular notice?" asked the Coroner.

"No. I was discharged at a moment," answered Mr. Arnold.

Mr. Evans said, "The Committee of the Club is composed of colliers. They refused to allow him to go on the Club and in consequence of that they would not allow him to work again. Since that time, he has gone round the county obtaining subscriptions to aid him getting tool as a tinman. We have subscribed".

Mr. Arnold handed the subscription list to the Coroner who read the name of the firm as a subscriber.

"They could not have thought very ill of you", said the Coroner, "The pity is that the underlooker, somewhat harshly ,said what he did the other day. However, he has withdrawn it and this, no doubt will appear publicly as the other. I am sorry it had occurred, but this is all we can do. I think I need not go into the matter further".

"I think Mr. Arnold will stand no worse before the public", commented Mr. Higson.

"I am sorry it took place ," said Mr. Billinge.

Mr. Peace addressed Arnold, "Does not your petition at the head of the subscription list say that you left because your memory was impaired and that you were unable to get employment at the colliery?"

"Yes, and I expected that was the reason why I was discharged but I could never get to know".

"It was not for giving evidence that you were discharged?" asked Mr. Higson.

"Not that I know of".

"You never thought so?" asked Mr. Driffield.

"No", replied Arnold and there the matter was finally laid to rest.

Mr. Samuel Cook of Haydock, who was the underlooker at the New Boston Colliery, one of the Haydock Collieries was the next to give evidence to the court. He said that he reached the

Dead Horses.

colliery about half an hour after the explosion and that he took an active part in the operations to recover the bodies from the Nine Foot Mine but he had not gone into the Six Foot Mine. He described the positions in which the bodies were found and the manner in which the search was directed. He thought that the explosion had taken place in Pilkington's brow. The force of the explosion had gone from this place in two directions and then forward to the workings below. He said that he had found exploded powder cans in both brows but in his opinion the main explosion had been caused by firedamp. He believed that the fall in the brow had caused the build up of gas and in ignorance of this fall, and the absence of the firemen, the men fired the shots which ignited the gas. The men were found blown against the coalface with their tools. He stated that in the December explosion, which occurred in a different part of the mine, had no connection with this explosion.

When questioned by Mr. Higson he stated that the men could not have known of the fall in the brow and he commented that, unlike the gas that he usually found in the workings, the gas that he encountered was hot. Mr. Pickard said that he found no gas when he inspected the workings.

Mr. Christopher Fisher Clarke, of Garswood, mining engineer to Sir Robert Gerard, was the next witness. He made two inspections of the colliery, one on 26th, July and the other on the 30th. July. On both occasions he went into the Nine Foot workings but he had been in the Six Foot Mine on the evening of the explosion. He had previous knowledge of the Nine Foot workings since his employer was a lessor of the mine. He thought that the blast had come up the west brow, along a tunnel and into the east brow. He commented on the force of the explosion as the worst he had ever seen and there was little signs of burning in the brows. He also thought that the blast had ignited the powder cans and in his opinion, the only way in which the gas could have accumulated was because of the fall. There would have been a cavity there from the last fall and in this the firedamp could have accumulated. The only possible reason that the gas had ignited was that it was passing when they fired the shots.

The Coroner asked Mr. Clarke about the point raised by Mr. Mercer concerning the lamp that had been found with a hole in the gauze. Mr. Clarke said that almost every lamp that he been recovered had a hole in the gauze, the damage caused by the force of the explosion. He now thought that the hole in the lamp in question was a rivet hole.

Questioned by Mr. Higson as to the source of the gas, Mr. Clarke referred to the evidence of the torn up rails on Pilkington's brow that indicated that the fall had occurred before the explosion, unlike a small fall on Parfett's brow under which the rails were damaged. The fall in Pilkington's brow was thirty feet in length, ten feet wide and three feet thick. this could have held a large amount of gas and he saw no evidence of negligence in the fact that the gas had not been detected.

Mr. Clarke made some comments on the ventilation of the two mines. Under the circumstances he thought that he ventilation system could not be improved. He had seen the colliery develop. The Six Foot Mine was the first to be worked, and from that the Nine Foot mine was reached and looked on as part of the Six Foot workings. In this context, he could not see the possibility of altering the ventilation.

The foreman said that the explosion could not have been prevented even if both firemen were on the scene but had there been a separate shaft to the Nine Foot workings then the mine would have been safer.

Mr. Peace pointed out that when the upbrows were completed they would have the effect of providing a separate ventilation system in the same way as another shaft would and Mr. Clarke agreed with this and said that the digging of the upbrow was the speediest away to achieve this.
"And the cheapest?", asked Mr. Higson.
"Both cheapest and quickest." replied Mr. Clarke.
Mr. Pickard asked Mr.Clarke to justify to the court the present system of ventilation and asked him if he thought it would be safe to carry on working in the Nine Foot Mine.
"Yes," said Mr. Clarke, "Until the upbrows are completed, I would justify the carrying on of the returns from the Nine Foot Mine, into the Six Foot Mine as at present. Had all gone right, I have no doubt the ventilation would, before this, have been carried by a shorter route. When the Nine Foot was first reached, a pair of brows were started towards Legh pit, but after carrying them forward for some distance, it was found impossible to carry on, but these that were then started are now being carried on".

When questioned by the Coroner about the explosion he answered, "I do not think that there were two explosions. I do not think that the coal is making gas in Pilkington's brow for in that neighbourhood the gas must have been well drained. The fall that I have suggested as to the cause of the explosion, might not interfere with the ventilation sufficiently to call the attention of the men working to the stoppage of air".

Mr. Dickenson, the Government Inspector for the Manchester, area then questioned Mr. Clarke with reference to the place referred to by Mr. Finney and Clarke said that he disapproved of allowing gas to stand in old workings of the mine but he thought that this had had nothing to do with the explosion.

Mr. Clarke stood down and Mr. John Chadwick, the underground manager of the Haydock Collieries, took the stand. He had held this post for fifteen or sixteen years and was a very experienced and respected man. He told the court that the Nine Foot Mine had been worked at the colliery from December 1865. The seam had been reached through a fault in the Six Foot workings and at another point in the mine at the same time. It had been the aim, from first entering the Nine Foot, to have a separate ventilation systems and since the December explosion every effort had been made in the mine to achieve this aim. The one hundred and fifty yards of tunnel that were referred to by James Finney as having been worked with bratticing, was driven as a ventilation tunnel and not to get coal. Extra care was taken with the work and special instructions were given to Mr. Chadwick who had personal responsibility over the work and his sole objective was the safety of the mine. He went down the pit as necessary and was always available to consult with the underlooker. It is well to bear in mind that work was going on in the mine to improve the system of ventilation to the method recommended by the Inspector following the December explosion and that this work was carried on at night with coal being mined only in the day.

With regard to the explosion, Mr. Chadwick agreed with Mr. Clarke about the possible causes. Questioned by the Coroner he said that he knew of gas in the workings which were in such a bad state that it was not possible to ventilate them.

Mr. Dickenson asked about the fall in Pilkington's brow and Mr. Chadwick said that six to eight hundred cubic feet of gas could have accumulated there, enough to have caused the explosion. Mr. Dickenson then raised the important point about a circular that Mr. Higson had sent to all the mine owners in his district when he asked if Mr. Chadwick had received a circular from Mr. Higson about the amount of powder used in mines and he was told that Mr. Chadwick had not but he went on to say that the colliers were allowed to take enough for a days use and no more according to the Colliery Rules. The coal in the mine was very hard and it took three men a day to get down one head from the face. As was made very clear later Mr. Dickenson that he did not think that powder should be used but the system of working the coal in the mine was one that he had not seen before. The Coroner suggested that the question should be discussed later and the sitting was adjourned but the question of the circular is one of which we shall hear more.

The Court assembled on Thursday 6th. August and there were dramatic scenes before the proceedings began. Before the examination of the witnesses, Mr. Higson asked the Coroner's permission to make some remarks and addressing the Coroner he said, "I really have no right to ask any questions in this court, only subject to your order, I really do hope that if I get irregular, you will correct me. I do not like the murmurs coming from the other side, murmurs of disapprobation. we are not legal gentlemen, we have no legal training as lawyers. We simply make this inquiry with the best possible intention and we are desirous to bring all the evidence before the jury, who are sworn diligently to inquire into the cause of death. I say that hardly any question can be considered irrelevant to the inquiry, Now, Mr Dickenson, at the last meeting stated a very proper question. It was a question with regard to gunpowder; if he had not brought it forward, I should have done so myself; and I hope he will have the opportunity of cross examining the witness again, because it is clear to me that gunpowder had to do with the last calamity in the pit, and the question therefore was a very proper one".

The Coroner asked, "Has the point ever been raised as to whether the question was irrelevant?"
Mr. Peace replied, "I have not in the slightest degree intimated anything".
"I am not allowed here to mention anything that has taken place outside, " said Mr. Higson, "Neither are the jury allowed to take notice of what is said outside. They are here to hear the evidence given before this court and are to form their opinions on that. I hope you will pardon me for making this remark. I had an object and it will have it's effect in the end".
The Coroner replied, "I am quite certain it would not have been made if that had not been the case. Personally I am not aware to what the illusion refers. With respect to the evidence of Mr. Chadwick, in the middle of which we stopped, on the express condition that Mr. Dickenson should continue his cross examination today".
"And Mr. Chadwick is in attendance for that purpose today", said Mr. Peace
"The question of gunpowder is very important and I hope it will be inquired into," said Mr. Higson.

At this point the jury was sworn in and the foreman of the jury raised a point which again brought drama to the Court when he said, "Allow me, Mr. Coroner, to say a word or two regarding to what Mr. Higson spoke about. It is at the express wish of the jury that I do so. They think that there is a tendency to check our questions. They may appear irrelevant and not worth answering to people learned in the inquiry and acquainted with all the technical terms used but the jury do think so and they think they ought not to be checked or made ridicule in any way".
"I must ask you for an explanation or request you to stop", said the Coroner.

Finding the Body.

"To explain what?," said the foreman.

"To what your remarks refer. They are irregular and I may tell you at once, but perhaps you will say to whom you are referring as wishing to stop the questions, for I have not seen it".

"You have tried yourself in any instances, Mr Coroner".

"I must stop these observations. I have tried to conduct the inquiry to the best of my discretion and judgement and I can not allow any more of these remarks, which are decidedly irregular".

"It is at the express wish of the jury that I have mentioned the matter", said the foreman.

"I think, as you say, your remarks bear upon those of Mr. Higson. I must call upon him to whether any of his observations referred to me".

"None what ever," said Mr. Higson.

"I can not imagine how they could," said the Coroner.

"I will explain, if you will allow me," said Mr. Higson, "When I was cross examining witnesses at the last sitting, I several times heard Mr. Peace distinctly murmur what I thought was disapprobation. I do not know if they intended me to hear, or for the jury, or for the witnesses. I felt it to be really annoying and I thought I would take the opportunity of naming it. Now I have said all that I desire to say".

"So you see Mr. Foreman, Mr. Higson's remarks had no bearing upon any interference in the part of the court.

"I thought that you disapproved of the question I put", said the foreman. "Bear in mind, Mr. Foreman, that form this moment the Court can not be interfered with. The Court takes it's own course; in doing so it incurs all responsibility, and it is not responsible to you".

"Then, as far as I understand, if you consider our questions are not bearing on the evidence, and upon the explosion, then you will stop them?"

"It is quite for you to say".

"That you will stop them?"

At this point the Coroner got a little rattled and replied,"Or suggest they are not carried forward is certain. I think I have stopped nothing at this inquiry, and I have no hesitation in appealing to every gentleman present to say whether I have done so or not. The number of days during which this inquiry has been going, will, I think, be sufficient to answer to any supposition of this kind. I might have commenced and concluded this inquiry in strict legal course in two days and I have no hesitation in saying that the amount of evidence of a strict legal character, and I need not have allowed any other to be heard in this room, need not have occupied more than two day and then the inquiry may have been stopped by me. No power could possibly have interfered with it and I might have put the matter before you and called for you to return a verdict, instead if that I have kept it open that every possible bit of evidence that could be brought before you and this should be appreciated. The only attempt to interfere or stop questions, I am aware of having made. have been when a lengthened cross examination had been going on in the case of a witness whose evidence upon the points in question was utterly useless and worthless when you heard it. For instance ,when engineering questions were asked of a man who could not read and write his own name. Upon that ,you must understand, that I have the fullest discretion and it is for me to say if a witness is unable to give evidence on the point put to him and to stop it. If also, after I have put the question to a witness and obtained a distinct answer, and the question is reputed, then I may stop it. In fact, as I have said before, you must leave all the questions of that kind entirely to the discretion of the court it's self. It is responsible for the course pursued, and not you".

"As far as I can see, we are like automats sitting here, " said the foreman, "listening to only what you consider right to be heard".

"I have said nothing of the kind. I have never taken a totally different view of it. It has never been suggested by me that you are anything like automats. In case I had closed the inquest in a couple of days, you would not have had the opportunity of cross examining witnesses and of suggesting why. In this instance you have had every assistance, you have had every witness called who you have suggested".

"I hope, Mr. Coroner, you will make every allowance for our not understanding the matter. Doubtless you are well acquainted with the subject".

"I am sorry to say, that as far as your remarks have gone, you make no allowance for my understanding of it. You say, in one instance that you do not understand it, and then you are actually dictating to the Court what should be pursued".

The foreman said, "Allow me to make one further remark".

The Coroner interrupted, "These proceedings are clearly irregular and had better cease. I have reason to believe that we will get through he main portion of our inquiry today. If the engineering evidence, including that from Her Majesty's Inspector is not gone through today, I fear we shall have to adjourn to a distant day. It is therefore exceedingly desirable that we should get on with the work without loosing time".

"I was going to observe ———", said the foreman.

"I would rather hear no more. This is decidedly irregular. I am sorry it had passed. I have only said what is necessary to face with the knowledge of those who, with yourself have been so ignorant as to the position of the court in the matter. I do not think I have put myself forward unjustly or beyond what has been called for in the immediate circumstances of the case. If I have done wrong I am ready to answer for it".

Mr. Peace then spoke, "Will you allow me to say, Sir, that I have never had the slightest intention, as I think you must have seen, that any of my remarks should allow the slightest tendency or desire on my part to check questions or interfere with the inquiry in any way.

I am not aware that I have and any murmurs if dissatisfaction. Unfortunately we sit at each side of a very narrow table and I have constantly have to be prompted by the scientific gentlemen besides me."

The Coroner, wanting to get on with the inquiry, said, "I should like this to stop; but with regard to what has been said by Mr. Peace I may just say that I never observed it. Mr. Higson may have done so. when this discussion commenced I really was not aware to what Mr. Higson alluded when he made his remarks. I have no doubt that, coming from where they did, he thought them necessary."
"I perfectly appreciate your indulgence in this and many other occasions, Mr. Coroner. There is an end of the matter", said Mr. Higson.

Following these diversions, Mr. John Chadwick was recalled to continue giving his evidence. In answer to the questions about the use of gunpowder in the mine, he said that the coal very hard and that the blown can that had been found in Pilkington's brow contained twelve pounds of powder. Mr. Dickenson asked about the practice of cutting the coal with the use of powder and John Chadwick told him that he had not seen the practice before he came to the Haydock Collieries but he knew that it had taken place in collieries in Parr and the Wigan district for the past fifteen years. Mr. Dickenson did not like this practice as will become evident later. He thought it a very dangerous way to get the coal. Up to this time the coal in the other seams that had been worked in the Haydock Collieries was much softer and could be undercut with a pick, then cut vertically and levered off the face with crowbar and wedges. The coal in this seam was very hard and could not be brought down without the use of powder. Holes were drilled into each side of the coal face and charges inserted and fired, hence the expression 'cutting the coal from both sides' and a lot of powder had to be used.

Mr. Dickenson asked him if he had introduced the practice to the Haydock Collieries.
"No." replied Mr. Chadwick.
"But you permitted it?".
"Yes."

Mr. Dickenson, who was very much against the used of gunpowder for getting the coal down from the face, then said that he did not think that Mr. Higson condemned the use of powder enough. He had said some hard things about it but they were not in strong enough terms for Mr. Dickenson. He then asked Mr. Chadwick again about the practice, and received the reply that the practice went on in the Manchester area, which was Mr. Dickenson's area.
"I am not aware of a single instance. If you will kindly mention at the close of the inquiry where it is to be found, unless it is discontinued, I will enter into an arbitration with the employers. I will not permit it to be practice in my district if it is within the power of the law to stop it. Will you tell me when you got the practice, Mr. Chadwick?"
"When from? It has been the practice in the district and the neighbouring district for years."
Mr. Chadwick went on to say that it was used only where the coal was hard to get. Mr. Dickenson pursued the subject and the Coroner asked if powder had anything to do with the present explosion. Mr. Dickenson said that he thought it had. Mr. Chadwick again stated that the cavity in the roof could have held enough firedamp to cause the explosion.

Isaac Billinge was recalled and he expressed his belief that

Pilkington and Smith had fired the shots that caused the explosion and that the shots had been fired in the presence of the fireman.

Mr. Booth, a mining engineer from Chadderton near Oldham was the next expert witness to be called. He had inspected the mine after the explosion on behalf of Evans & Co. and he thought that the gas came from the fall. He also approved the method of ventilation of the mine. Mr. Dickenson asked about the method of getting the coal and Mr,. Booth said that it was a practice that the had not met before and therefore he could not comment.

Mr. Joseph Dickenson, the Government Inspector for the Manchester area was then called as a witness. He had made an inspection of the mine at the request of the jury and the approval of the Home Office. He thought that there could have been one thousand cubic feet of gas in the fall that had been repaired in Pilkington's brow and that the powder tins throughout the mine had ignited, giving a much more devastating effect to the explosion. He thought that the ventilation could have been weakened at a critical moment due to the furnace at Legh Pit dying down a little or possibly a ventilation door being left open and he stated that he had found some dirt behind some of the doors in Queen Pit. He saw nothing wrong with the ventilation system of the mine but again returned to the question of the use of gunpowder in the mine when he went on to give a detailed argument of the reasons he did not approve of powder being used to get the coal.
"The way in which powder is used in this pits, is in my opinion, very reprehensible. I call it an abuse, not use," he said.
"Do you mean the quantity?", asked the Coroner.
"The large and unnecessary quantity, making the powder do the work that should be done by the pick. By this system as much powder is used in a day as would be used in a week in a proper system and we find that we have explosions."

"In consequence?" the Coroner asked.

"What might have been only a flash of gas and affected a few men, becomes a great explosion. The mining engineers who have been smiling at the statement that powder had to do with these explosions can only be smiling at their ignorance for they have no idea of the manner in which it had been used in this district".

Mr. Peace pointed out that there was ample power under the Mining Act to enable the Inspectors to take steps to stop the practice and that the men objected to any restriction since they had to earn a wage that was based on their output.

Mr. Pickard asked if it was safe to work the mine under the present practice and it was agreed that it would be safe to do so.

Mr. Peter Higson, the Government Inspector for the area was the next witness. He was in the mine after the explosion had taken place but he was unsure as to the seat of the explosion, other than it was one of the two brows. commenting on the use of powder in getting the coal he said in his opinion more was being used that was desirable but he did not think that it was a factor in the explosion. He went on to say to the court that in 1867 he had received a letter from the Miner's Agent, Mr. Pickard, complaining about the state of the pit. He had mentioned this letter neither to Mr. Evans nor Mr. Chadwick but he had visited the pit and spent three days inspecting the workings but he did not find anything of which to complain about except the practice of letting the return air pass over the furnace. On receiving his recommendations a dumb drift was constructed in accordance with the Inspector's wishes.

With regard to the use of powder in the mine he said that he knew of collieries in St. Helens and Wigan where no powder was used at all and others that used a very large quantity, "as to put themselves, their workpeople and the public in very great danger". He went on to say, "Gunpowder is stored in Scholes in Wigan, to such an extent that I should not be at all surprised to hear that the whole of Scholes be burnt down".

With reference to the comments of the Inspector for the Manchester area he said that the extensive use of powder was due to the nature of the coal, it being very hard and compressed. On a visit to the colliery with Mr. Pickard he had tried to get the coal down with a pick and found that it was impossible. Mr. Pickard interjected that it could be got down, but not in such quantities that a collier could make a living.

Mr. Peace then put the Inspector on the spot when he asked Mr. Higson, "Are you prepared to stop all the collieries in your district from getting coal in this manner?".
"I have not said so".
"But I ask you if you will do so".
"I do not think that I am bound to answer that question," replied Mr. Higson.

Mr. Peace seeing the point as vital to the interests of Messrs. Evans and Co. appealed to the Coroner, "He said that the sole object he had for making the inquiry was to ascertain whether the practice, said by one inspector to be dangerous, would put a stop to it".

The Coroner reminded Mr. Peace that Mr. Higson had not stated that the practice was dangerous.
Mr. Peace then said, "Then I ask the question to Mr. Higson. Do you think the practice of getting coal without cutting one side should be stopped?"

"I do".

"And believing that, will you take such steps as are necessary for putting stop to the practice?"

"So far as it affects the colliery concerning which we are making this inquiry".

"Do you mean to say that your circular will affect this colliery alone?"

"I did not say anything of the kind".

"And will you answer the question?"

"No."

"Do you know that such a state of things exist in other collieries in you district?"

"I have heard that such is the case".

"Can you tell me if you have ever had a letter from a mine owner specially asking you to serve a notice on him to stop holing in this way?"

"I don't remember".

Mr. Mercer, the proprietor of the Park Lane Collieries, Ashton-in-Makerfield, interrupted, "I suppose Mr. Peace is referring to me".

There had been two explosions at the collieries that had caused loss of life a little time before. The cause of the explosions was the fact that large quantities of powder had been stored underground.

"I have had no such letter", said Mr. Higson.

"I believe that you did not comply with the request concerning the system of blasting?"

"I did not".

Mr. Dickenson said, "Now, for the guidance of the jury as to whether this practice is to be continued and say whether you make any recommendations in the future".

"With regard to this. Sir", said the Coroner, "I do not think Mr.

Higson has any business to commit himself here".

Mr. Higson replied, "I thought I had stated distinctly that coal should be got at one side before the shot is fired and that the quantity of powder taken down the mine should not exceed two pounds per man".

"For the satisfaction of the jury, will you state that you will not act partially to one colliery, and that what ever steps you may take, will have reference to all?", asked Mr. Dickenson.

"I am not going to tell either Mr. Peace or Mr. Driffield or the jury or yourself what I am going to do. If I found a colliery in which there was no gas being made, it would be unfair to stop blasting there as in the same way it would be in a fiery mine".

The foreman of the jury said, "From what he have heard here, this seems to be one of the safest mines in the district. There is nothing to be found from one mine explosion to another".

"But there was an explosion in the mine in December, "replied Mr. Higson, "And another six months afterwards and it is a black spot on it's escution".

Mr. Peace again asked Mr. Higson if he would state whether he would try to put a stop to the practice in other collieries and to say if he proposed issuing a circular on the subject.

"I will tell you nothing unless these matters are connected with the inquiry," said Mr. Higson.

"I hope this will be taken notice of by the press", said Mr. Peace, "I think it is very unfair that Mr. Higson should adopt this course to one colliery alone".

"Mr. Higson has said nothing to cause you to ask for this purpose from him," said the Coroner, "If Mr. Dickenson, who made the statement as to the danger of the practice had been before you, the matter would have been difficult, but I do not think that Mr. Higson had stated anything strong enough for you to justify you in

Body on Trolley.

requesting such a pledge".

Mr. Higson said that he could not understand why the matter had been pressed so far. Mr. Peace said that it was a very serious matter to the proprietor of the colliery. If the practice had to be stopped at the colliery alone, there would be a possibility of not getting men to work at the pit.

Ralph Dearden, the furnace tenter at Legh Pit was the next witness to be called and he stated that he was on duty at the time of the explosion and that the furnace was working to it's full capacity at the time.

The sitting was then adjourned until Tuesday and the jury told the Coroner that they were anxious to hear the evidence from the Miner's Agent, Mr. William Pickard. Mr. Pickard said that he would be present at the next sitting of the court.

The sixth sitting of the inquiry opened on Tuesday 9th. August with William Pickard, the Miner's Agent, being the first witness. He had inspected the Nine Foot Mine after the explosion and he was of the same opinion as Mr, Higson as to the seat of the explosion, it was in one of the brows, but he did not know which since he had found indications in both of them. He did not believe that any of the falls of roof, not even the one in Pilkington's brow, had occurred before the explosion. He thought that the quality of the timbering that had repaired the roof, was so good that it could not possibly have fallen under the circumstances and that only the blast could have dislodged it and caused the timbers to fall. He found ventilation doors that had been left open in the Nine Foot Mine and this could have weakened the ventilation which did not dilute the gas that was given off the coal. He stated that he disapproved of the ventilation air being led from one mine to another.

He thought that the practice of blasting the coal from both sides would call for extra ventilation and this was not provided at the pit and he said that the effects of a one and a half pound charge could have serious effects on the ventilation.

He was then closely questioned by Mr. Higson about the practice of blasting coal from both sides that was carried on at the colliery. He asked, "Is it general practice in this district in getting coal from both sides?"

"I have heard of it of late. The men ought to be remunerated in cutting one side so as to render it unnecessary", answered Mr. Pickard.

"Where is the practice followed?"

"I have heard of it at the Pearson and Knowles collieries but there is little gas given off there and the mines are well ventilated".

Mr. Higson went on, "Did you know that the Nine Foot Mine was one of the most fiery in the district when it was first opened ?"

"Yes. I heard Mr. Cook the underlooker at the New Boston Colliery say that when it was first tapped, the Nine Foot gave off so much gas that it was possible to use it".

"If this is a fiery mine, and we have heard from many witnesses that it is not, ———,"

"I differ with them", said Mr. Pickard.

"If it is not," continued Mr Higson. "It is natural to suppose that this calamity would not have happened?"

"Quite so."

"That it is a fiery mine is proved by the fact that gas had been in the old brows for seven months and cannot be removed?"

"It is".

"Now, with regard to blasting, I should like you opinion because active measures have to be taken and your support will be wanted. We can not have men killed in this way. In the first place is it safe for men to work in a place where it is not safe to blast even two shots at a time?"

"It is not safe. I do not approve of men working where it is not safe to blast."

The Corner asked, "Do you mean that it is not safe to work a mine where gunpowder is used?"

"No.", said Mr. Higson,"What I meant was as to whether it is safe to allow men to work in a mine like this, where it can not be safe to blast".

"But does that not amount to what I suggested?", asked the Coroner.

"Where no part should be worked when the coal should not be blasted?", said Mr. Pickard, "But I meant to say that it can be ventilated so that you can blast in safety".

The Coroner went on, "But you know that here a large number of the Arley Pits in which blasting is prohibited and yet men are getting coal there. Do you condemn that? It is generally considered safe to work in these pit because no powder is used? I think I have stated the legal effect of Mr. Higson's question though I am sure he means something else".

Mr. Higson said, "What I desire to ask is this, if the ventilation of the mine is not sufficient to allow men to fire shots in his working place, is it not safe for a man to be there at all?"

"I say it is not," said Mr. Pickard.

Mr. Dickenson took up the questioning of the witness at this point and began by saying that Mr. Pickard had stated that he Nine Foot Mine was second only to the Arley Mine in danger and in the account of his exploration he had said that he found no part of the mine making enough gas to account for the explosion. He went on, "It has been stated that half the explosions in the district are caused by colliers drinking over night. Do you think there is truth in that?" Mr. Pickard answered, "I believe it has an affect on management and precaution when men are in the habit of drinking. In the present instance I do not believe that drink, either on the part of the officers or the workmen, has anything to do with it. With the Hindley Green explosion, on the contrary, drink was seriously mixed up".

"If half the explosions were caused by drinking overnight ———".

"I do not admit that assertion, " interrupted Mr. Pickard.

"You have not contradicted it."

"I believe that drink had a serious effect on the officers and servants and that it may more or less lead to negligence upon examination".

"Take it this way," continued Mr. Dickenson, "If drink is to such an extent mixed up with these casualties, how is it then, that the men in this district are more given to it than others?"

"I can not say, " said Mr. Pickard. "When I used to take drink, I was only too glad to sit down on the slack-heap and rest. I could not do my work, my head was too heavy. If a fireman however neglects his duty through drink the result may be more serious".

"Then you think this more serious to officers then to men?", asked the Coroner.

"Of course. The fireman are compelled to go down but the men may take a day of rest. I think, however, that there is no need to complain about the judgement of Mr. Chadwick in this respect. Yates I knew to be a steady, sober man and as far as I know, Billinge also".

"But is it not the custom in other districts for colliers to go a whole week without a drink? Are there peculiar circumstances leading to consumption here?", asked Mr. Dickenson.

"I can not understand it," said Mr. Pickard, "The Associations of men are the same everywhere. I should like to see the officers of the collieries freed from all association with local drinking customs which, unhappily, are too prevalent".

"I agree with you that there is too much on sale everywhere, Mr. Pickard. That is my experience, " said Mr. Higson.

Mr. Dickenson then asked about the shot firing. "Do you as a practical man, consider it safe to fire such a heavy shot?"

"I do not. I have never heard of such a large quantity of powder being used at once. I believe that a man who had given evidence once fired four shots at a time."

"Who was that ?", asked Mr. Higson.

"Finney".

The Coroner said that he would be recalled. Mr. Dickenson went on, "Do you approve of the old custom of cutting from one side?"

"Yes, if the men are remunerated properly. I believe that since the explosion, Messrs. Evans & Co. have prohibited a number of men blasting in the Main Delf. The remuneration that they offered was insufficient, six pence per yard, and the men would not accept it. At the Norley Colliery a dispute arose from the same cause and there was a stoppage at Hindley Green".

"Could coal be got in this mine without powder?" asked Mr. Higson.

"I think it is possible without blasting, by the use of hydraulic pressure".

"But not under the present circumstances and with the present appliances. Is it possible to get coal without blasting?"

"No. The Masters could not compete without the use of powder".

"Are you aware , that for the last thirty years, the practice of blasting from both sides has been used in the Wigan district?"

"I am not. I have only had knowledge of the mine for five or six years".

Mr. Higson commented, "Mr. Chadwick has told us that it had

been the general practice throughout the district. I have found a case in Wigan district where it has been practiced for thirty years and that is in a mine that makes as much gas as any in the country and still it has never lead to a casualty".

Mr. Pickard commented that blasting depreciated the value of the coal since it made a lot of small coal for which there was only a limited market at the time.

Mr. Dickenson stated that, in answer to a previous request, Mr. Chadwick had given him the name of three collieries outside the district where the practice was carried on and on inquiry, he found that two out of the three blasted the coal but the masters disapproved of the shots bring fired from both sides. One side had to be cut. When this was practiced, the owners were anxious to give it up but were hampered by it going on in the Wigan district and as the collieries were in Blackrod they could not see how they could compete in the market unless the Wigan pits also changed their practice". He continued, "They are willing to give up the practice if the others join them. One colliery undertook to try three places with cutting from one side for a month, and I wrote last night to the other asking it to do the same. I have no doubt that they will do it. The quantity of powder that they use does not approach the quantity used here. I know of no instance where one pound is used and very rarely is three quarters of a pound exceeded".

Mr. Higson spoke, "What may be done hereafter is besides the inquiry. The question is what, before the explosion, was the general practices. I entirely disapprove of any opinion being offered or comments made as to what should be done. I do not know myself what power I have. If the practice complained of prevails over the whole of my district, I can not arbitrate with every colliery owner."

"Certainly", interrupted Mr. Peace.

"The arbitration clause is not worth the paper on which it is written," said Mr. Higson. Mr. Higson made this remark from bitter experience when he had experience of the process of arbitration under the Mining Act a few years before concerning the closure of a St. Helens colliery which he thought would be left in an unsafe state and he lost the case since the system was biased in favour of the coal owners.

He continued,"It was in contemplation some time ago to amend it to a short Act of Parliament. I would not fight the battle without stronger powers which I have under the present Act. I, some time ago, anticipating casualties like this, issued a circular to each coal proprietor in the district in which I said :-

"The great loss of life from the unskilled use of gunpowder clearly proves that blasting in mines which emit inflammable a gas, should at once, be discontinued for getting coal. In those mines which do not give of gas, it should be allowed under competent supervision."

I had previously submitted this to the Home Secretary. He ordered it to be printed and it was distributed as I have said, a copy to Mr. Evans and to Mr. Mercer and all the coal proprietors in the district. I was in hope, until the recent explosion, that greater care was being taken in the use of gunpowder. Not a single reply reached me from any quarter and I consider it was incumbent on the colliery polarimeters to discontinue the use of powder in fiery mines. In every case that comes before me, I mean to have the question tried. I will summon every colliery owner before the magistrates. If they were anxious to avoid accidents, the case had been placed before them. The time for arbitration has passed. I am not, however going to say what I will do in the future but I have prepared a further circular to the colliery owners in my district which I shall ask the Coroner to read".

The Coroner said that he would read it, but in the meantime, the Court should proceed with the examination of the witness.

Mr. Pickard took the stand and in reply to a question from Mr. Peace he said that he could not say and did not know the differences in pay between the colliers in the Six Foot and the Nine Foot Mines. Mr. Peace asked, "Are you aware that Messrs. Evans & Co. do not allow any fireman or underlooker in their employ or any of their officials to be in any was connected with any public house or beer house?".
"I did not know that any such rule was in existence", commented the witness, "It is highly commendable on the part of Evans & Co."
"Do you know that Mr. Higson, in his report on the Haydock Collieries dated 28th February 1869 said that:-

"Although the mine makes gas, it can not be called a fiery mine, and it can not be worked without gunpowder' "
"I have seen the report and I believe that was in it."

Mr. Higson spoke, "You seem, Mr. Pickard, to attach some blame to some person for this calamity. Would you kindly give us your opinion of whom that person is?"
"I think you ought to ask him first if he does blame anyone", said Mr. Peace, "He has not yet said that he does".
"I say that certain circumstances have occurred but I think it not for me to say who is responsible. I have told you what I can with regard to the accident", said Mr. Pickard.
"Do you blame the fireman?", asked Mr. Higson.
"If the cumulation of the gas was sudden, I would not blame the fireman for he might have been engaged in some other part of the

mine with duties that required his attention".

The foreman asked about the exploded powder can and Mr. Pickard said that this could have aggravated the disaster but he pointed out that it would not have blown if the gas had not fired at the same time.

The Coroner asked if any other witness were to be called and Mr. Peace said that Mr. Gilroy and Mr. Byrham, both mining engineers who could not come before the inquiry before were now in court. The Coroner said, "And I was of the impression that it was because of their absence that Mr. Booth was called. These gentleman have, however, viewed the pit and if you desire to call them you can do so".

William Byrham, mining engineer of the Rose Bridge Collieries, Wigan was then called. He generally approved of the system of ventilation and thought that the gas had been liberated from the fall in Pilkington's brow. The cavity should not have been there. It should have been filled or ventilated and that was the only fault that he could find with the mine. It had been ignited at the top of the brow. He thought that the gas was more likely to have been ignited by a faulty lamp than by a shot.

In reply to further questions from Mr. Higson, Mr. Byrham, related that recently, in one of his mines. a twenty six pound can of powder had accidentally exploded and on that occasion no damage was done what so ever even though there was a man ten yards away. If he had worked at Queen Pit, he would have fired shots at both ends.

George Gilroy was the next mining engineer to be called. He was the manager of the Ince Hall Coal and Cannel Companies

Collieries. He thought that the gas had been liberated by the fall, which he was sure, had taken place before the explosion. He said that there was no danger of firing two shots at the same time and Mr. Dickenson said, "I have heard it stated that you are the father of the system of firing shots without cutting."

"That I will demur altogether. I think it is an innovation of late years but it is not one that is made by me. It is made by the colliers themselves because I am sure no owner or manager cares for it being done. They would prefer it cut because it may be got in a better manner".

Mr. Dickenson pressed the point. "Taking the system as it is practice where, a shot at each side, one and a half pounds of powder in each, do you feel yourself disposed as to the father of it?"

"Certainly not. I have never practiced it under circumstances similar to these".

"Then, from what I gather, you do not approve of it?"

"I see no objection to the practice of it in this mine."

"Why in this mine more than others?"

"The coal is very hard at the bottom and very difficult to get without shots on both sides but powder may be abused in a way I have pointed out:.

"And if it is liable to abuse, should not the system be avoided?"

"As far as an employer can control his men, he ought to advise them to lay shots so as to avoid the likelihood of fast shots, in the way described. I think a smaller quantity of powder would suffice."

"If this mine is so exceptional, that it requires such large shots, would it not be better to discontinue working it and let it take it's turn rather than force it into the market before it can be worked at the market price?", asked Mr. Dickenson.

"Speaking of leaving mines in the ground, some of us would be very glad to do so but, unfortunately, the inferior mines which are often connected to the the hardest, are connected in the leases with superior mines, and in some, leases was are tied down to current working".

"That is so".

"And these are presumably of the inferior class?"

"In the Wigan district, the Wigan Nine Foot is so assumed", answered Mr. Gilroy.

"But surely as hard as it is at Haydock?".

"No".

The question of leaving the coal that had been found until there was the technology to mine it safely is an interesting question. We have heard that the Nine Foot coal at Queen pit had been found by accident and there was obviously a great deal of pressure in the form of demand for coal that mining operations had started.

In answer to the further questions from Mr. Dickenson, Mr. Gilroy again stated that he did not think that the gas had come from the cavity as it was not large enough to hold all the gas that had caused the explosion and that if the gas had been found by Mr. Chadwick and Mr. Billinge, they would have taken steps to remove it at once.

On the question of explosives, Mr. Gilroy thought that there was too much powder in the mine.

"And too much to be fired?", asked Mr. Dickenson.

The Coroner interrupted and said that Mr. Gilroy had already told him that he thought that the system was open to abuse. This ended the examination of Mr. Gilroy.

The Coroner asked Mr. Higson if he had any final remarks on the case or upon the evidence that had been given.

"I want to say a few words to the jury before you charge them," said

Mr. Higson. "At the close of the last sitting, a question was put to me which I did not, at the time, think that it was proper to answer insomuch as it was, in my opinion, travelling out of the course of the inquiry. I did not decline from any disrespect to you, Sir, and going home very much distressed at an expression of Mr. Evans, that I was acting an unjust part. I think my character is too well known in the district ——".

"Allow me, Mr. Higson," interrupted the Coroner, "to say to you, to confine your remarks to what has occurred in the court. Nothing of that sort had occurred in my hearing".

Mr. Higson continued, "I wish to put in evidence the circular note I sent to all parties in my district, Mr. Evans, Mr. Mercer and everybody I could think of. I did not get a single reply from any quarter. I consider I have drawn the attention of everybody in the country to the unskillful use of powder in getting coal in this part of the kingdom. That is quite as much as I could do at present, for the circular was sent out in the middle of last year and it travelled far and wide.

Now, as to the question of compelling everyone in the district, to discontinue the use of powder. I do not think I could accomplish such a thing for years to come without Parliamentary powers. The Coroner says I must not travel out of what I have heard in court, but I really am obliged. I could not arbitrate under the Act, with any confidence of success. I have heard three of these arbitrations and I can not say that any one has been successful, while the last was a complete failure and now the parties are actually trying all the suggestions I have made to them before the arbitration commenced.

What would the public think of an inquest if Messrs. Evans had the powers of appointing you as jurymen as they have the power to name all the men who are to arbitrate? How can it be expected otherwise that all my endeavours should fail?

I have written to the Secretary of State, asking him to carry a short Bill this session prohibiting gunpowder altogether without his sanction, I wrote to him last night. I don't think he can do such a thing, but I am showing him how strongly I feel on the subject. Long before this circular and before this casualty happened, I tell you I had anticipated events.

I do not know that I have much to say to you except one or two remarks on the evidence. With regard to the evidence of the colliers that this confined gas had exploded or caused the explosion, I entirely disagree with it. I can have no such thing".
"What confined gas?", asked a juryman.
"The confined gas in the old brows. It has been ignited in one of the two upbrows and whether it accumulated in the cavity spoken of by one or two witnesses or fouled behind the brattice in the brows, I think, impossible to say without accuracy, but I will take another question. Whether it has come from the cavity in the roof? Mr. Byrham has told you that it ought to be ventilated and these men, Yates and Billinge. They were paid to look for accumulations of gas in the hole above. both behind the brattice and every where else, as the Special Rules of the Colliery state, that if a fireman found gas, they shall have it removed and stop the men working"..
"But none had been found", said the Coroner.
"I do not connect, Mr. Evans with the explosion. Mr. Evans said that if he was asked for ten thousand pounds to make the pit safe, he would have found it. I believe it and I believe he would have given double the amount but surely this is not the natural state of things.

This must have been caused by some neglect. We know that gas will accumulate in mines and we employ these men to see that the gas is carried away harmlessly. I have found men in Lancashire that remember when there was no brattice. In my early life, in Mr. Dickenson's district, there was a very large colliery in which no brattice was used at all, although the mine was fiery. They cut through every ten yards. That, however, was found to be dangerous and now brattice is used to conduct the ventilation fifty or even a hundred yards.

As with gunpowder, I can hardly tell the jury the extent to which brattice is abused. Many mines in East Lancashire do not require gunpowder".

"It is extensively used though", said Mr Dickenson, "In the Clifton district, it has continued for twenty years. It is extensively used, but not in the quantities used now. It is never used, except in deep workings and then not frequently".

"That shows that the custom of the district changes, " said the Coroner.

"I speak from experience", said Mr. Higson, "It was my own act and deed for twenty one years. The cleavage of the coal enabled men to get it down with a hammer, wedge and crowbar. It is not so in this mine and it takes a great deal of labour to get it down without powder. Mr. Pickard will also tell you that these places should be safe before shots were fired. If these places are safe, then the only injury there can be is from gunpowder. Mr. Byrham tells you he has known twenty six pounds of powder being fired by a man ten yards away. I know of this happening in the Buckley Colliery in Mold".

"I do not know what verdict you will find, but it is my duty to explain the facts. If there had been no gas in the mine there would have been no explosion. We can only connect it with gas accumulated somewhere and it is your duty to say who neglected their duty and allowed the gas to accumulate".

The foreman asked, "How are we to arrive at the knowledge

whether the circular was received?"

"It is not the matter. It had nothing to do with our purpose here today", said the Coroner.

"I have the book in which I took all the names of all the parties to whom I sent the circular", said Mr. Higson.

"It is no part of the inquiry", said Mr Driffield, "It is only to show that Mr. Higson has not neglected his duty and to show the steps he had taken since the last explosion".

"I sent the circular and no reply came. I therefore took it for granted, as it was natural to suppose, that I should, that everyone agreed with it. I have further proof in my pocket that it has been received."

Mr. Dickenson said, "You say in your circular:-

The great loss of life from making the use of gunpowder, clearly proves that blasting in mines which emit inflammable gas should be discontinued for getting coal. In those mine that do not give off gas, it should be used under competent supervision.'

"You intend that as a recommendation to coal proprietors to be careful in all events. More careful than they have been hitherto?"

"They are to use every possible care," said the Coroner.

"You are telling us to believe that they have not carried out your instructions?", said Mr. Dickenson.

"I am stating nothing of the kind", said Mr. Higson.

"He is only telling you what he has done", said Mr. Driffield.

"Mr. Peace put the question to me at the last sitting;- 'Will you compel every coal proprietor to do the same thing, this is to discontinue the use of gunpowder on both sides?'

As there was and expression of discontent, I thought that I would carry what I had done further and I have now issued this circular throughout the district:- *"Swinton, Manchester. August 6th. 1869.*

Sir, I beg to call your attention to my circular letter transmitted to your place a few months ago, including my remarks on the improper use of gunpowder and brattice in working mines. I have to inform you that yesterday it was stated at Haydock, that at a large majority of collieries in my district the practice of blasting without cutting from one side or end was still continued. This, having been the customary mode of working at many places at which the most recent painful calamity caused great loss of life, and if it not be abandoned may be the means of still greater fatality. It is now clearly proved that the men are allowed to take down the pit, at a time, unnecessarily large quantities of gunpowder inadequately secured. I have, therefore, to request that you will inform me in reply, if these practices exist at your colliery and in which mine. I have also to suggest that the members of the coal trade should meet, arrange some well considered scheme (therafter to be adopted throughout the district) and transmit to me within a month, for the purpose of removing the evils now so widely complained of. I shall avail myself of all authority and power I can obtain in this quarter,
    I am, Sir, your very obedient servant,
    Peter Higson.

Mr Peace asked, "Your first circular was issued on 1st. January 1869?"
"Yes".
"And I observe in you report dated 21st, February in speaking of the Haydock explosion, you say:- 'That although the mine was making gas it can not be called a fiery mine and can not be worked without the use of gunpowder.'".
"Yes. Due regard being given to the character of the mine".
Mr. Peace continued, "I wish to show that you did not intend your first notice to prohibit the use of gunpowder".
"I said I did not consider the mine a fiery one, Now circumstances

have altered. I should call a fiery mine one that has had gas confined in to for seven months which all efforts of the management can not remove".

The Coroner said," I have now to request from you, a suggestion or two on behalf of myself and the jury with regard to recommendations.

You yourself have said that we should have to make one or two recommendations and I think you gave us to understand that you would have to agree to these suggestions or we would have no hope of carrying them out into effect. I have to ask you to now make these recommendations to the jury to consider".

"I should certainly recommend an increase in the ventilation and should discontinue taking the air from the Six Foot Mine in to the Nine Foot Mine".

"How should this be done?", asked Mr.Peace.

"I should restrict the use of gunpowder and cause the place to be ventilated. The judges have distinctly laid down that every part of the mine should be ventilated. The owner should give distinct attention that this should be done. They themselves do not go down the pit to examine the workings. They do not know, except from report, whether the workings are well or ill managed but they provide money not to say abundantly but extravagantly as they have also done to do anything for ensuring the safety if miners. The jury should further recommend, though they can not impress on the men,a thing about which they are not personally satisfied, the total discontinuance of blasting if machines can not be produced to do the work".

The foreman asked, "Suppose blasting is carried on. We will allow that if necessary. Can it be done at the time when the mine is not filled with men? "

Mr. Higson replied, "Mr. Mercer is doing that now. I believe the shots are fired at night when the miners are absent. Two men are allowed to go down the mine for that purpose. They hold their lives in their hands. They do not fire any charge if they think there is danger and no one can fire a shot except themselves. So far the regulation is good."

"This is in the Arley Mine", said the Coroner.

"Can the men working on this plan get fair wages?", asked the foreman.

"Just the same as any other place ", said Mr. Higson.

"If Mr. Mercer's plan is practical then I think it should be adopted", said the foreman.

"It may be practical in some cases but not in others", said the coroner, "You can ask Mr. Higson if he is prepared to support such a recommendation if you make it".

"That is what we want to know".

"Well, yes." said Mr. Higson, "I would recommend the improvement of the ventilation and the ventilation of the two mines made separated. The more ventilation be provided and the quantity of powder be restricted and the coal cut down on one side before blasting. We will regulate the rest ourselves".

The foreman asked, "What would be the effect upon the extravagant use of gunpowder by the miners if the powder was issued to them by the proprietors?"

"That can not be done", said Mr. Higson, "because legally the proprietors can not make deductions from the men's wages for powder or anything else".

Mr. Dickenson said, "The decision of the Queens Bench Court in a Scottish case laid it down for as far as Scotland was concerned the stoppage for powder and other such articles could legally be made".

Mr. Peace commented. "I beg to say that this is not the English Law. There has been no decision".

The Coroner began his summing up and outlined to the jury

what happened during the sittings of the court. He spoke for about half an hour and then asked them to retire and to consider their verdict. They were absent for about an hour and forty minutes before returning the following verdict:-

"We find that Joseph Edwards and fifty eight others came to their deaths from an explosion occurring in the Nine Foot Mine at the Queen Pit, Haydock on 21st, July 1869 last and that the explosion was of firedamp caused by a shot igniting the gas brought from a fall in Pilkington's place and we are also of the opinion that the explosion was aggravated and the loss of life considerably increased by the quantities of gunpowder in the mine. We further find that if proper care had been taken to remove the gas in the cavity in this fall, the explosion would not have taken place. We recommend that the coal should be got in the manner spoken of by Mr. Dickenson, that is, cutting on one side and that further blasting operations shall be carried out at night in the absence of the workmen. We also consider it objectional for the Nine Foot air to be returned through the Six Foot workings."

The Coroner said "There is only one matter requiring explanation, namely, whether you consider the explosion a matter of accident or wish the point to be left over".

"If you consider that the accumulation or outburst of gas from the roof was of an unexpected character, it would be only fair that you say so", said Mr. Driffield.

"The jury think it ought to have been known that the gas was there. Whether the fact was known or not we can not say", said the foreman, "Then you wish the matter to be left over?"

"Yes. We do not want the have the words 'unexpected or accidental' inserted in the verdict".

The verdict was duly recorded and the Coroner thanked the jury for their services and at this point the proceedings were terminated.

REPERCUSSIONS OF THE JULY
EXPLOSIONS.

The inquest was widely reported in the National Press of the time and had an effect on Victorian public opinion. The issues that emerged from the Queen Pit inquiry prompted opinions to be voiced.

A strong editorial in the Wigan Observer dated 20th, August underlined many of the important issues that had been raised by the inquiry and concentrated on the circular that had been sent to all the mine owners in the district by the Government Inspector. The circular had additional importance since it had been submitted to the Home Secretary.

There was no doubt that it had been distributed but there was reluctance on the part of the owners to say that it had been received and little evidence that it had been acted upon. Mr. Higson issued the circular to show that he was doing his duty and all that his office had allowed him to do to achieve this end.

The proprietors of the Haydock Collieries made no secret that they had received the circular and Mr. Higson had assumed that all the owners of the district had acted on the circular but, as the July explosion had shown, that they had not done so. By his statement that Evans & Co. would have spent ten thousand pounds to prevent the calamity, it can be seen that the Inspector had every confidence in the proprietors of the colliery but the dangers of taking large quantities of gunpowder into a mine that gave off a lot of gas and the indiscriminate blasting of the coal in a pit where there had been an explosion six months before had obviously not been fully realised.

There had been a series of causes that had led to the explosion. In the first place there was firedamp in the mine, then the questionable ventilation system that was used in the colliery and finally the use of powder to get the coal. The verdict found that there was gas, powder and blasting, but the verdict did not find, as it should, that the use of powder in a mine that gave off gas should be discontinued. At the very time that a meeting of mining delegates in Manchester, that was attended by Mr. Pickard, had petitioned Parliament for an inquiry into colliery explosions. The Editor of the 'Observer' thought that the practice should have been discontinued.

The paper thought that the verdict was a strong one but not strong enough as to satisfy the mining community of the country as a whole. The 'Observer' did not think that a verdict that implied criminality should have been returned since the men who were most to be blamed had been killed in the explosion, but in the view of the paper, Mr. Higson had foreseen circumstances leading to the second explosion and that was to his credit.

Much Parliamentary time had been taken up with the question of the Irish Church and the Mines Regulation Bill had been neglected. A draft Consolidation Bill had been brought in which was an attempt to focus the laws but not to change them. What was required was a short Act which gave the Government Inspectors power to issue orders to the owners subject to an appeal to the Home Secretary. The editorial pointed out that if it had been the case in 1868 then fifty nine lives might have been saved and the second explosion prevented.

Many National Newspapers ran articles on the repercussions of the explosion and the 'Times' commented that the jury did not like to say that the accumulation of gas in the cavity was due to neglect and they wished to leave the matter open. The 'Times' thought that the verdict threw a serious reflection on the men who were responsible for the mine and that if the jury had been prepared to say that there was neglect, then criminal proceedings would have to be taken against those thought to be responsible.

In due course, changes were made in mining practice and the Inspectors given more powers of compulsion over the owners. The hard lessons learned from the loss of the lives of the men and boys in the Queen Pit explosions took many years to find their way into the general mining practice in the coalfields of the country.

POSTSCRIPT.

The lessons learned by the explosions took many years to find their way into the mining legislation and it was not until very much later that a safe explosive was discovered for use in mines, until that happened, underground shots were still fired but under much tighter control. The pattern of work changed in most pits with the blasting down of the coal taking place at night when there were few men down the pit and the main workforce working during the day to prepare the coal for blasting.The quantity of powder that was taken down the mine was limited and the manner in which it was carried was carefully regulated.

It took years for the Inspectors of Mines to have the powers to compel mine owners to make changes in mining practice and lives were still lost underground from explosions of firedamp. Messrs. Evans & Co. restricted the use of powder in the Haydock Collieries and altered their working practices but even so at the Wood Pit in Haydock in 1878 in a mine where there were no explosives used, there was a great explosion that caused the deaths of about two hundred men and boys.

It is sad to note that Mrs. Hindley of Old Boston, Haydock who lost her husband, Joseph and her son, Henry in the December explosion at Queen Pit, lost three of her sons, Joseph, James and John in the Wood Pit explosion of 1878. Thomas Reed who identified so many of the victims of the July explosion was also a victim of this explosion.

Finally, Isaac Billinge, the underlooker at Queen Pit who was gassed, blown up, led the rescue operations in the December and the July explosions as well as loosing a brother in the latter and took a leading part of the underground operations following the Wood Pit explosion, retired from the service of Richard Evans & Co. in 1889. He died peacefully in his bed in October 1892 aged sixty six after a full and eventful life in the Haydock Collieries.